# 40 Years of the Best

# Contemporary Doll Stars

featuring
Fashion Dolls:
Barbie®
Alexander
Celebrity

**by A. Glenn Mandeville**

Published by Hobby House Press
Hobby House Press
Cumberland, Maryland 21502

# Dedication

This compilation would not have been possible without the untiring devotion and help of my best friend, Robert Gantz. An artist by trade, and photographer par excellence, Bob helped turn inanimate objects into "living dolls." Through many a crisis his cool head and professional attitude helped quell the creative beast that lives within all who see more than an object through the lens. The balance of our talents made these works possible.

Edited by Virginia Ann Heyerdahl

Additional copies of this book may be purchased at $14.95
from
Hobby House Press, Inc.
900 Frederick Street
Cumberland, Maryland 21502-1298
or from your favorite bookstore or dealer.
Please add $3.30 per copy for postage.

ISBN: 0-87588-385-0

# Introduction

Collecting dolls has long been a hobby enjoyed by many. It has only been since the early 1970s, however, that the collectors of dolls made from the 1930s and on have been recognized as "legitimate" members of the doll collecting world.

An incredible amount of knowledge has come to light during the past fifteen years. Individuals have come forward with rare company catalogs that show exactly what dolls were available, and for which years. These have been an overwhelming help to the doll researcher, and even to the novice collector.

Many authors began to write about collecting modern dolls in the 1970s. With their pioneer work, others were able to contact former employees of major toy companies. Often these individuals had taken with them samples, or even "rejects," and many times invaluable prototypes of designs not utilized. As writers and others locate and interview these "links to the past," we finally were able to piece together most, and sometimes all, of the information about a particular company or a specific doll.

Collecting modern and collectible dolls has changed a great deal over the past two decades. Prices have risen and fallen, risen again, and demand has fluctuated greatly as publicity generated more interest in dolls. Some "closet" collectors were so overjoyed to discover that others shared their interests that their entire lives were changed. Often, entire families now collect dolls in some form or another, and men as well as women boast of some of the finest collections to be had.

As we look back on the past two decades, some notable and baffling things occurred. The Coleco Cabbage Patch craze of 1983 was something not likely to be seen again, where normally sane individuals fought in stores and parking lots to buy a chubby faced, yarn haired doll. Collectors of Madame Alexander dolls were limited to two dolls per person in some stores in the late 1970s, prompting disguises and family and friend accomplices in order to buy more dolls!

The *Barbie*® doll, around since 1959, has become the largest selling doll of all time, with sales at 800 million dollars alone in 1991! Special *Barbie* dolls are now being created in porcelain as well as vinyl, and the collector is seen as a vital part of Mattel's customer base.

The thirtieth anniversary of *Barbie* in 1989, led to publicity that has attracted literally thousands of collectors, sending prices upward in a seemingly never-ending spiral.

One must also mourn the passing of Madame Beatrice Alexander at the dawn of a new decade, but her dolls, in my opinion, will always remain the standard by which all dolls from the "Golden Age," the 1950s, will be judged.

Finally, one cannot help but notice that the newest part of our doll collecting hobby is the emerging group of contemporary doll artists and their following. From about 1980 on, many talented individuals have come forth and not only reproduced dolls from the past, but have initiated new methods of doll making that seem to know no bounds.

As a lifelong doll collector, and full-time doll dealer, I am proud to help the collector sort out the many facts and ideas presented to him/her. My column, "Dollars and Doll Sense," and my many articles in **Doll Reader**® magazine, have allowed me to reach a vast audience with new ways to look at old friends, and has given me a chance to introduce many new ones as well.

I know you will enjoy this compilation of articles, and whether you are seeing them for the first time, or reading them again, I am proud to present to you this selection.

Knowledge is *always* the key to enjoying any hobby, and I know that many facts presented here will assist you in your doll collecting. I am thrilled and delighted that my shared knowledge will help all of us appreciate and love our hobby even more!

# Table of Contents

Introduction .................................................3

## *Barbie*®

The Takara *Barbie* Story ...........................6

The *Barbie* Look, Part I: (1958 to 1963).......11

The *Barbie* Look, Part II: (The Couture
  Period [1964 to 1966]) ...........................18

The *Barbie* Look Part, III: (The Mod Period
  [1967 to 1971]) ....................................24

The *Barbie* Look, Part IV: (1970 to 1988) ....30

Flying High with *Barbies* ..........................36

Goin' to the Chapel with *Barbie* ..................42

## Contemporary

Dolls Like Girls — The Evolution of
  *Katie*™ A Living Portrait ...........................51

You! Boys and Girls Forever: Takara
  Company's Lifelike Children ....................56

*Jem*™, Beautiful or Truly Outrageous,
  Part I ...............................................62

*Jem*, Beautiful or Truly Outrageous,
  Part II .............................................70

Brooke Shields — She's A Doll ..................78

The Alexander Doll Company — An
  American Tradition Continues ..................82

Lady Luminous, A Japanese Doll Dresses
  Up .................................................88

**Above:** A rare number one brunette *Barbie*® modelling *Gay Parisienne*. Read the article "The *Barbie*® Look, Part I," for more information (pages 11-17).

**Front Cover Photograph:** *Braniff Welcome Abroad* suit. Read the article, "Flying High with *Barbies*®," for more information (pages 36-41).

**Title Page Photograph:** *Tippi* by Madame Alexander. Read the article, "The 1980s — A Decade of Dolls on Review," for more information (pages 130-137).

**Back Cover:** Left photo: *Shirley Temple* (see pages 130-137). Right photo: *Tippi* by Madame Alexander (see pages 130-137).

Starr™ and Her High School Friends ............95

The 1980s — A Decade of Dolls on
    Review ............................................102

*Kimberly*® — A Play Doll Turns
    Collectible ......................................109

Black Fashion Dolls of the 1970s and
    1980s ..............................................114

# 70s

*Cher*® — A "Sing"ular Sensation .................120

Rare and Unusual Collectible Dolls .............130

# 50s and 60s

The Many Faces of *Ginny*® ...........................138

So Beautiful Her Name Just Had to be
    — *Revlon*® ....................................146

*Twiggy*® — The MOD Model ......................154

Ideal Dolls — The End of an Era ................161

The World of Alexander-Kins......................168

35 Years with *Betsy McCall*® .......................174

The *Chatty Cathy*™ Story ............................180

The *Mary Hartline* Story .............................186

Index ..........................................................190

One-of-a-kind mint-in-the-box *Shirley Temple*. Read the article, "Rare and Unusual Collectible Dolls," for more information (see pages 130-137).

# The Takara Barbie. Story...

It certainly is no secret to *Barbie* collectors that Mattel grants licenses to various companies to produce *Barbie®* and *Ken®* for foreign markets. Sometimes, Mattel itself manufactures these dolls with the ethnic features of that country. Other times, the names "Barbie" and "Ken" are purchased by manufacturers to make their own version of this famous duo.

It has been known for some time that *Barbie* and *Ken* items were available in Japan. Mint-in-box outfits from the mid to late 1960s have surfaced here from time to time, and so have some very strange dolls! *Illustration 1* shows *Living Eli*, a friend of *Barbie* made in Japan in 1970. She is made from a unique mold, with huge eyes and pointed nose, and is on a *Living Barbie* body. The catalog shows *Barbie* and *Eli* wearing and sharing clothes. Apparently *Eli* did not catch on because she was only on the market a short time. *Barbie*, however, continued to sell in Japan in similar versions to those sold here, like the *Superstar Barbie* in *Illustration 2*. According to company records, *Barbie* was not a big seller in Japan. The Japanese, frankly, did not like the quality, and her large breasts and overly sexy manner offended many Japanese parents. The polished sophisticated image Mattel had cultivated here for their doll did not fit in with the Japanese culture in the late 1970s.

In the early 1980s, *Barbie* was not issued in new versions, and it looked like she would be discontinued. Around that time a Japanese company, Takara, had been manufacturing high quality dolls in Japan. Their fashion doll, *Licca,* was beautifully made and detailed. She was made here in a cheaper version (under the name Lisa), because the American consumer would accept lesser quality. The company had a New York office, in the Toy Building, and remained active in the manufacturing of robots and other high quality boys' toys.

Suddenly, in 1981, collectors traveling to Japan found something startling. A new *Barbie,* made by the Takara company! This new doll was breathtaking. She embodied the way the Japanese saw our teenagers. This *Barbie* had long straight blonde hair, big brown eyes, and her accessories were real, not molded plastic. The quality of this number one Takara *Barbie* was astounding. The doll, shown in *Illustration 3,* came with a lovely poster, photographed professionally, that stated, "Your friend came from America." On the packaging were also the words, "American Girl," and "Barbie is a fashionable American gal." Her innocence and joy of life could be seen quite plainly. This was definitely more in line with *Barbie's* image here 15 years ago. Collectors were thrilled, but the best was yet to come!

Soon high quality dolls and accessories flooded the Japanese market. The Japanese pre-teens, eager to have any contact with Western culture, elevated *Barbie* to cult status. Stores were hard-pressed to keep stock of the new dolls. Teens copied *Barbie's* dress and manners in their zest to be "Americanized." *Illustration 4* shows a greeting card done in the most simplistic style, yet the "American Girl" graphic tells all...*Barbie* WAS becoming "your friend from America." She embodied all that was RIGHT about the United States: Part "Valley Girl," part wealthy, part sweet, part sexy...this new *Barbie* told an idealized tale of teen life in America. In fact, the American collectors soon became even more obsessed with the new *Barbie* just for that reason. The fantasy life she portrayed was obviously not real to us, yet we WISHED it were. The Japanese thought it WAS true, and thus began *Barbie's* fullfillment to all who adored her!

Interestingly, Takara treated *Barbie* as an American icon of fashion. Their Excelina Collection, the top of the line, featured blue-eyed dolls, the only dolls with this color eyes! (Perhaps they thought blue eyes were more of an American ideal.) *Illustration 5* shows the richness of the clothing. Pure wools, 100 percent cottons, real suede and velvets were used on these dolls.

Like most companies, Takara became frightened that their success would diminish. During 1982, they experimented within different directions, like the doll in *Illustration 6, Romantic Barbie.* Very overdone, and not American at all, she was quickly discontinued. Finally, by early 1983, the identity of *Barbie* as a sweet, high school girl was cemented in place. Wonderful themes such as *Illustration 7, Sweet Country Barbie* evolved. Each doll came with a professionally photographed booklet that a real fashion model would envy. Real cloth flowers were used for trim, instead of the plastic ones here.

**Illustration 1.** *Living Eli,* a friend of *Barbie,* made in Japan in 1970.

**Illustration 5.** *Barbie* wearing clothes from the Excelina Collection.

**Illustration 6.** *Romantic Barbie.*

**Illustration 7.** *Sweet Country Barbie.*

7

Gradually, with the advent of MTV and other American pop and rock tours, Japanese youths began to see American teens as living like the stars of "Fame"...a freewheeling life with no responsibilities, yet working toward some sort of unidentifiable goal. Stars such as Madonna left a mark on Japanese youth, who were eager to shed some of the traditions of their culture, especially those which had held women in bondage. *Illustration 8* shows three influences American culture had on this doll, a doll frankly billed as representing American women. The first is *Candy Pop Barbie*, definitely TODAY, with her wide leg stance and raised arm, body language that denotes freedom and confidence. The second doll to me definitely reflects the "Dynasty" influence, for even the hair is in Linda Evans' style, cropped at her shoulders. The third doll, *Fruits Kiss Barbie*, portrays a timeless "Carmen Miranda" costume look, so popular in our culture. These dolls, even more so than the *Barbie* of the 1960s here, tells the story of American fashion and fads, better, because it is seen from outside our culture, and focuses on the ideals that our television shows and magazines portray.

**Illustration 8.** *Candy Pop Barbie, Barbie* again wearing clothes from the Excelina Collection reflecting the "Dynasty" influence and *Fruits Kiss Barbie.*

Finally, in 1985, *Barbie* had really gone "New Wave," as Japanese designer Yamomoto Kansai designed a series of coordinate clothing for *Barbie.* Like his real-life designs, this doll's clothing is high quality at its best. The sneakers are painted with details, and the designs on the sweats are applied separately, not drawn. These garments are so perfect that they would please the pickiest of fashion addicts!

*Illustration 9* shows a *Kansai Barbie,* now with cropped hair, in an octagonal shaped box.

Not to be overlooked is the traditional *Japanese Kimono Barbie, Illustration 10,* with resplendent kimono, sandals and fan. The details of this costume are stunning and models for each season are available.

Perhaps the most interesting thing about the Takara *Barbies* is the photography and the design of the packaging. The Japanese take great pride in their work, and each *Barbie* design is laid out perfectly. *Illustration 11* shows the pains taken to convey the image of *Romantic Barbie. Illustrations 12* and *13* show the exquisite Fur Dress Collection boxes, with graphics and photography equal to those of a Bloomingdale's catalog. *Illustration 14* shows

**Illustration 9.** *Kansai Barbie.*

**Illustration 10.** *Japanese Kimono Barbie.*

just a simple package back for a nightgown, yet every detail in the photograph is perfect. In fact, all the Takara items ARE perfect, making collecting these accessories most rewarding to the collector who thought quality was finished.

The many varied outfits such as the Coordinate Dress Collection shown in *Illustration 15* are unbelievable. The tiny stereo included is so real one expects to hear music playing. The Japanese Stewardess outfit, complete with poster in *Illustration 16*, is tailored like the finest garments. The little director's chair leaves no doubt as to who the "star" of all this is...and the guitar with real strings can almost play "Barbie is a Fashionable American Gal"...a legacy true here for 26 years... and now the Japanese know it as well.

Note. Because of licensing agreements, Takara *Barbies* are not sold in America. It is illegal to import them for resale. Collectors desiring these dolls should ask relatives and friends going to Japan to get items for them. Watch the trade papers for collectors selling duplicates. Try to cultivate a Japanese pen pal, and learn about Japanese culture while continuing your doll collection! These exciting dolls are just one more reason to get involved in the doll "world"! □

Barbie® and Ken® are registered trademarks of Mattel Toys.

Illustration 12. One of the exquisite Fur Dress Collection boxes.

Illustration 13. Another of the exquisite Fur Dress Collection boxes.

Illustration 11. An example of the pains taken with photography and the design of the packaging to convey the image of *Romantic Barbie*.

Illustration 14. The package back for a nightgown.

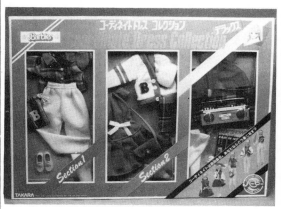

Illustration 15. Outfits from the Coordinate Dress Collection.

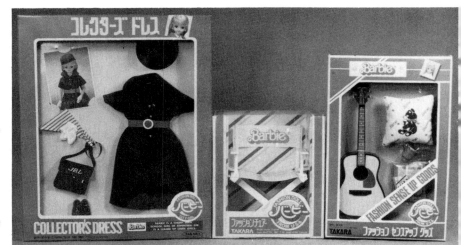

**Illustration 16.** Japanese Stewardess outfit, director's chair and guitar with accessories.

**BELOW: Illustration 17.** The Takara *Barbie* and *Ken.*

**Illustration 1.** A rare number one brunette *Barbie* made at the Japanese factory without much supervision was shown at Toy Fair in 1959. *Barbie* models *Gay Parisienne*, a stunning "bubble" dress that is also very hard to find.

# The *Barbie*® Look, Part I (1958 to 1963)



This is the first part of a four-part series of articles which will highlight the creation of and chronicle the development of *Barbie*®, the world's most famous doll.

While working on my new book, *Doll Fashion Anthology and Price Guide*, featuring *Barbie*®, *Tammy*™, *Tressy*®, et al, (published by Hobby House Press, Inc.) so much information came to light about the creation of *Barbie*, and the various periods of her "life," that it soon became apparent that there were just too many facts for one book! During my interview with Ruth and Elliot Handler, in February 1987 (after they received the prestigious "Lifetime Achievement Award" bestowed by Hobby House Press, Inc.), I knew that there were lots of "tidbits" that collectors would love to hear! Thus was born the idea for a series of articles that would complement the information in *Doll Fashion Anthology and Price Guide*. When combined with your copy of the book, the entire story of *Barbie*®... *Teenage Fashion Model* comes alive with these articles which will also feature all new photographs, as well!

Most doll collectors know by now the basic story of the creation of *Barbie*. Ruth Handler had watched her daughter, Barbara, play with paper dolls as a child. Barbara Handler complained to her mother that the glamorous world of fashion should be three-dimensional. Ruth and Elliot Handler together set out to develop such a doll. The end result would be the best-selling doll in history! Before *Barbie* actually entered the marketplace, there is quite a story.

In my interview with Ruth Handler, she denied any tie-in at all to the Bild *Lilli* doll from Germany. Some feel there is a connection, however, and

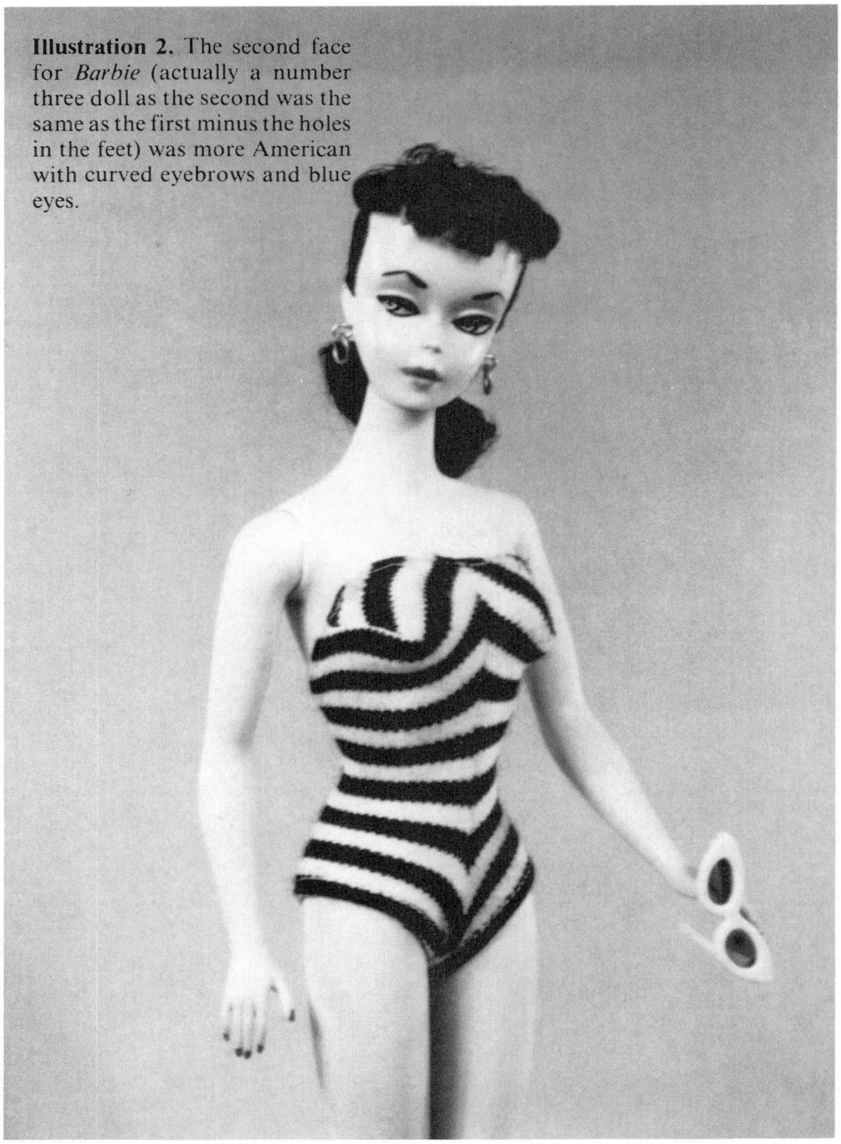

**Illustration 2.** The second face for *Barbie* (actually a number three doll as the second was the same as the first minus the holes in the feet) was more American with curved eyebrows and blue eyes.

*Tammy*® is a registered trademark of the Ideal Toy Corp.
*Tressy*® is a registered trademark of the American Character Doll Co.

**Illustration 3.** A richer, warmer vinyl was used on the number four *Barbie*. Her hair is still a soft fiber. In my opinion, this is the most beautiful of all the ponytail *Barbie* dolls.

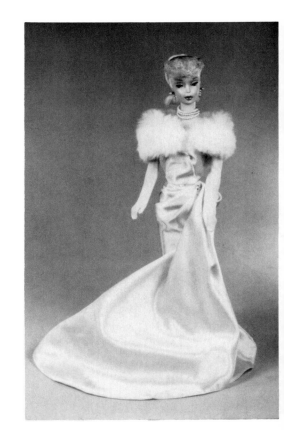

thus already here is the first mystery concerning the creation of *Barbie*. Elliot took Ruth's plans to Japan, where mass-marketed toys were made much more cheaply than here in the United States. Without Ruth's supervision, a prototype was made. In fact, several prototypes were made up. Some had very Cleopatra-like eye makeup. Others had red hair, while some had no bangs to the hair style. Elliot brought home THE prototype that would be the number one *Barbie*. Ruth was not pleased, but deadlines had to be met. They had already booked space at Toy Fair that year (1959), and the doll had to be shown. The "bugs" could be worked out later. Ruth and designer Charlotte Johnson were hard at work on the fabulous wardrobe for *Barbie*, which they felt was more important than the doll. It was then that Ruth, who was a marketing genius, decided that the concept for *Barbie* was simple. It was the beginning of a new decade. A time of peace and prosperity. No wars, no depressions, just a glorious future to look forward to! New technology like television and airplanes were changing everyday life. Children WANTED to grow up. There was no

**ABOVE LEFT: Illustration 4.** Full-length view of number four *Barbie*, shown in **Illustration 3.** *Barbie* is modeling *Nighty Negligee*. This outfit featured a Grecian bodice nightgown and pleated peignoir. Accessories were high-heeled mules with pink pompons and a stuffed dog for her bed. The bubble bath was a licensed product for children.

**ABOVE RIGHT: Illustration 5.** Ads had to be made in advance so even this advertisement from the March 1960 issue of *Toys and Novelties* featured the doll from the previous year, a number one *Barbie*.

**RIGHT: Illustration 6.** A perfectly mint number five doll or, as Mattel calls her, "The Original *Barbie*" models *Enchanted Evening*, one of the great formals for *Barbie* during the early years. This doll and outfit were used in 1987 for the porcelain *Barbie*, called *Enchanted Evening*.

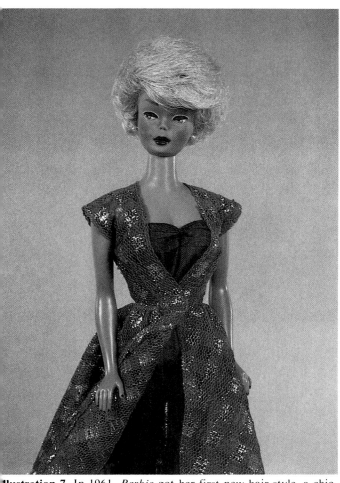

**Illustration 7.** In 1961, *Barbie* got her first new hair style, a chic "bubble cut." Made in a wide range of colors, it was available for several years and is the most common doll found today. *Barbie* is wearing *Dinner at Eight.*

**Illustration 8.** *Barbie* got a best friend, *Midge®*, in 1961. The same size as *Barbie, Midge* was happy to play a supporting role in all of *Barbie's* adventures. (*Barbie* is wearing *Career Girl*, while *Midge* models *After 5.*)

longer a reason to hide behind a mother and father. Sons did not have to go to war, and daughters could now go to college. The children of the late 1950s had a great chance that no other generation before them in the history of the world had!

"I designed *Barbie* with a blank face, so that the child could project her own dreams of the future on *Barbie,*" states Ruth. "I never wanted to play up the glamorous life of *Barbie.* I wanted the owner to create a personality for the doll."

After Toy Fair it became apparent that there were some problems. Buyers were not thrilled with the doll. It was too pale, and the white eyes were not lifelike. The stand, with its two prongs that fit into the feet, was hard to work (and costly to produce). All in all, *Barbie* had an overly grown-up look, and a "hardness" that was not appealing. The wardrobe, however, was stunning: real zippers that zipped, satin linings, the finest of accessories. The clothing was as well made as that of

real people! Not being manufactured domestically, it was obvious the Japanese took pride in details. The Handlers had a winner, but she needed some refinement.

By the next year, 1960, *Barbie* had gone through three transitions. First the costly stand was replaced with a round stand that had a wire section that fit under her arms. Secondly, her face was "Americanized." "Blue eyes are the ideal," says Ruth, and so the number three *Barbie,* was given curved eyebrows and blue eyes. Still, the doll was a bit pale, so a fourth model was issued in rapid succession that had a flesh tone to the vinyl. It is this ponytail doll, the number four doll, that is the "original" *Barbie.* Basically the first three dolls (and even the fourth to a degree) are just "samples," as they did not even last a year on the market. By the end of 1960, the bangs on *Barbie's* famous ponytail were changed to saran, a sturdier fiber. This doll, the number five type of *Barbie,* was the one that was mass manufactured at the rate of

6,000,000 a year. It is this number five doll that Mattel today in its publicity pictures calls "The Original *Barbie.*" While technically correct, it is this confusion of terms that causes great problems with collectors and sellers of these early dolls. All these dolls are marked with the Roman numerals for 1958 on their behinds. The "original" *Barbie* with saran bangs is worth about $50 to $75 in gently played-with condition, and is the doll most often found today. The other four dolls are really prototypes themselves, and worth anywhere from $1800 for a mint brunette number one, to $250 for a mint number four.

The creation of a personality for *Barbie* became inevitable and really crept up on the public. Despite Ruth not wanting this to happen, *Barbie... Teenage Fashion Model,* was changing from a projection of the child's identity, to a real live person with an identity of her own. A series of children's books were published by Random House that cemented the identity of *Barbie,* and by now, her boyfriend, *Ken*. In the storybooks, it was established that *Barbie* had a middle name (Millicent) and last name (Roberts), went to high school (Willows High), and had a best friend, *Midge*. *Barbie* was basically a shy, sensitive down-to-earth girl who was pretty, talented and popular, but it was all sort of just "there." *Barbie* became like Sandra Dee, in the sense that she was perfect in every detail, but unspoiled. By striving to be LIKE *Barbie*, a little girl learned how to be pretty and popular.

The critics of *Barbie* at the time, felt there was too much emphasis on materialism, and that the doll taught the wrong values. I disagree. Only by trying to be perfect and then falling short, do we grow as a person. Many girls I meet today tell me they never would have gone out for cheerleading, or run for class president, or vied for Homecoming Queen, if they had not had *Barbie* and her play value at these activities to serve as a role model. Like a person who claims a movie is too offensive without ever having seen it, the critics of *Barbie*, for the most part, were people too old to remember fun, or possibly denied it by the troubles of the previous generation. Anyway, the REAL critics of *Barbie* were little girls who adored her in such numbers that Mattel soon became the largest toy company in the world!

Soon a boyfriend was added to the line. *Ken..He's a Doll* appeared in 1960. Looking very like Troy Donahue, *Ken* did for many little boys what *Barbie* did for little girls. In my research for my book, and at countless doll shows, I am still overwhelmed by how many men owned *Ken* dolls as children. As a child, I bought my first *Ken* doll on the boardwalk in Ocean City, New Jersey. I immediately adored him and learned many lessons about how to be a young gentleman from him. *Ken* was the "boy next door," the type of young man who would always have the "right" manners, and yet would excel at sports, dancing and academics. He was my idol! Sadly, I also learned that the flocking on his head which looked so much like a real "crew cut," came right off when he went in the swimming pool with me! This led to the rapid release later that year of a *Ken* with a molded crew cut! It is this molded-hair *Ken* that is also the "original *Ken*" as the flocked-hair doll was in many ways a prototype.

The last interesting fact is really kind of an insight into the doll manufacturing world. We collectors today think that everything shown in catalogs is "gospel." We accuse dealers of not having the "right" parts on our "collectibles." The reality is that Mattel issued *Barbie* to make money! Today we hold her on a pedestal, but even the Handlers have trouble understanding why adults would pay so much for what was to them a child's toy marketed by their company to earn a profit.

Ruth explained that parts were used up until they were gone. That is why so many mint-in-box items have such variation. Also, if an outfit was made only one year, it was because it did not sell well. *Red Flair*, a gorgeous red velvet coat and hat for *Barbie* was made for several years because it was a popular selling outfit.

All of this is as it should be. Mattel was in business to show a profit, and it is not their fault that today we all are *Barbie* crazy!

Yes, my views on the creation of *Barbie* have changed a great deal. I have learned about economics, manufacturing and marketing. None of this has changed my mind a bit about *Barbie*! I still think that no toy in history portrayed the "American Dream" better than *Barbie*. The collector of *Barbie* is most fortunate. Through a collection of *Barbie* dolls and fashions, the entire history of a generation can be viewed in three-dimension. The early years of *Barbie* were quiet ones in our history and the fashions reflect that peace and prosperity. By 1963, the assassination of a President, racial unrest and political upheaval would show on the ever-changing face of *Barbie*, a face that would change and reflect the face of youth for the next three decades! Ahead lay "The Couture Period," and new friends and adventures for *Barbie*, *Ken* and *Midge*! □

**Illustration 9.** In the beginning *Barbie* had no definite personality, but as licensed products flooded the market, she soon took on the qualities of the ideal American teenage girl. Shown are record albums, jewelry, paper dolls and bath accessories.

**ABOVE: Illustration 10.** High school life was portrayed by *Midge* wearing *Senior Prom, Ken®* sporting *Tuxedo* and *Barbie* wearing *Campus Sweetheart*. The outfit names say it all! **BELOW LEFT: Illustration 11.** Naturally *Barbie* and *Ken* were well traveled. In 1963 a series of travel costumes took them around the world. Here they are in Mexico! The detail is outstanding. Each outfit came with a story booklet. **BELOW RIGHT: Illustration 12.** Every high school student dreams of having the lead in the class play! Here *Barbie* and *Ken* are *Guinevere* and *King Arthur*, part of the *Little Theatre Costumes* from 1963.

**Illustration 1.** A 1965 *American Girl Bendable Leg Barbie®* with ash blonde hair, models the high couture fashion *Gold 'N Glamour* from 1965. These dolls and fashions are the most sought-after by collectors.

# The *Barbie* Look, Part II:
## The Couture Period (1964 to 1966)

This is the second part of a four-part series of articles which will highlight the creation of and chronicle the development of *Barbie®*, the world's most famous doll. The first part of the series appeared in the April 1988 issue of **Doll Reader®**, pages 160 to 166.

By the end of 1963, American teenagers as well as America itself, had undergone many changes. The assassination of President John F. Kennedy had left its mark on many things. It had sombered up teens and their approach to life. Many were questioning the values taught in the 1950s.

On the brighter side, another role model of the early 1960s was now having a profound effect on fashion. That woman was Mrs. Kennedy, better known simply as "Jackie." Jacqueline Kennedy had been the closest thing this country ever had to a queen. Followed by "Ladybird" Johnson, these two women brought an elegance and a sense of grace and class to the White House and the nation.

The image of *Barbie*, now firmly cemented in the minds of the toy buying public, was also changing. An amazing thing was happening to the owners of *Barbie* dolls. They were simply NOT putting them away! Even in my own experience, girls in my junior high school, who thought themselves very grown-up and sophisticated, still purchased the lovely gowns and outfits for *Barbie* and proudly displayed the dressed doll in their rooms. *Barbie* had simply become such a part of their lives, that surrendering the fun was just unbearable.

Ruth Handler and Mattel had always had a keen marketing sense. They allowed *Barbie* to grow up. A special playset became available in 1964 called, *Barbie Goes to College*. It now allowed the high school girl who was STILL in love with *Barbie*, the opportunity to project even FURTHER down the "role model" path of

**Illustration 2.** A gorgeous 1964 *Swirl Ponytail Barbie®* in blonde, captures high fashion wearing *Magnificence* from 1965. Her regal look is one of class and sophistication.

**Illustration 3.** A stunningly made-up *Color Magic Barbie®* with ruby red hair from 1966 lets them all drop dead in *Matinee Fashion* from 1964.

**ABOVE RIGHT: Illustration 4.** Ready for the dance! *Allan®* wearing *Best Man*, greets *Midge®* in *Holiday Dance* from 1964 to 1965. *Ken®* escorts handsomely in *Tuxedo* a super rare side-parted flip *Bendable Leg Barbie®* wearing *Fraternity Dance* from 1964.

life to all the crazy, zany capers which filled the lives of college students.

One has to keep in mind that for many girls, this was the first time that ANY member of a family had had the chance at higher education, yet alone a girl! *Barbie* was definitely serving a place that mother simply could not in most cases, that of a role model of what a college girl should be like.

These sociological implications cannot be overlooked in the *Barbie* story. *Barbie* was being played with by older girls simply because she had not outgrown her original concept. She was, for many girls, the heroine they looked up to, and, quite frankly, no one else was around at the time, real or fictitious to fill those shoes!

Because older girls were playing with *Barbie*, quality had to be maintained. The Couture Period, 1964 to 1966, produced, in my opinion (and the opinion of most collectors), the most desirable and beautiful dolls and outfits. Ironically, many sellers of *Barbie* dolls and clothing today find that with a few notable exceptions, the 900 series outfits, made from 1959 to 1963, are NOT the valuable ones. Neither are the early dolls, with the exception of the number one, two and three dolls. It is the *Bendable Leg Barbie*, when never-removed-from-box, or mint, and the lovely 1600 series fashions from 1964 to 1966 that command top dollar. Unlike other dolls, such as Madame Alexander et al, the "heart" of the valuable and elusive items lies within the Couture Period.

Exactly what does "couture" mean? It means to me "tailor-made by someone of talent." It is a word that implies "classic" and that means "timeless." Many of the 1600 series outfits were based on real couture designed ensembles by such notable designers as Balenciaga, Dior, Chanel and Balmain and could be worn today! In fact, many of these outfits are often copied and this author knows many people in the fashion business who have "borrowed" some designs from *Barbie's* stunning mid 1960s wardrobe. Television stars such as Joan Collins on *Dynasty* often wear outfits that are really "costumes." This is the other element of a couture outfit. The wide-brimmed hat is lined in the same polka

**ABOVE LEFT: Illustration 5.** A *Bendable Leg Skipper®* from 1965 dressed in *Me 'N My Doll* from 1964. A very rare side-parted *American Girl Barbie®* from 1965 matches in *Dancing Doll* from 1964.

**ABOVE RIGHT: Illustration 6.** The joys of teenage life were accurately portrayed as *Fashion Queen Barbie®* from 1963 tries on her three wigs to get ready for a date.

dot fabric as the dress. The "costume" idea of dressing dates back really to Joan Crawford in *The Women*, a 1939 movie that featured a color segment (rare at the time) fashion show of "costume" like clothing designed by Adrian, THE top designer of the day.

Not all of the *Barbie* fashions from this period are "couture." Many are *Barbie* simply playing her role as the perfect college student. Names such as *Student Teacher, Modern Art* (a stunning green day dress with an oil painting done by *Barbie!*), *Fashion Editor* and *Fraternity Dance* all tell of a beautiful girl's natural progression to college life. Much the image that Dolly Parton projects today, *Barbie* had the look that belied the work that went into making her a success. It all somehow has the look of an "accident." *Barbie* just was the prettiest, the most talented and the best at whatever she did, but because she was so "unaffected," no one seemed to be jealous. Who could be jealous of someone that perfect, yet so open, vulnerable and down to earth. These are the same

**RIGHT: Illustration 7.** The updated packaging such as this for the *Bendable Leg Barbie®* showed a more grown-up image. *Barbie* was now in college!

elements that were in Bill Woggons' *Katy Keene* and, as mentioned before, Dolly Parton.

The famous Doctor Spock once wrote that "Conceit is the destroyer of success," and how true, for the word was never part of the *Barbie* vocabulary!

Progress came rapidly for Mattel during this time. It seemed that all other dolls fell down at the high-heeled feet of the *Barbie* doll! In 1963, *Fashion Queen Barbie®*, a molded head doll with three glamour wigs, was added to the line. (There is some overlap in the *Barbie* story that is unavoidable.) The adult image was being cemented further and further away from the Sandra Dee early days.

In 1964, even *Barbie's* signature ponytail got a new treatment with a wrapped bang front (called by collectors a "swirl") that made her look older. The makeup colors on the lips varied, from reddish-orange to pure white. Another role model that looked very *Barbie*, was the blonde-flipped Pat Priest, who was playing Marilyn Munster on *The Munsters*. (Few living then realized that the man whose signature was on their dollar bills, Ivy Baker

Priest, Secretary of the Treasury, was her father!)

The real magic in the life of *Barbie* was the introduction of *Skipper®*, *Barbie's® Little Sister*. Still part of the line today, *Skipper®* was modeled after the young owner of *Barbie*. Supportive, never jealous, *Skipper* was glad she had a sister like *Barbie*! This was the year (1964) of the lovely matching outfits for *Barbie* and *Skipper*. Extremely well-made with well-thought-out themes, these outfits took the girls everywhere together from the skating rink to ballet class. Now more children could be involved. Mattel, fearful of losing the next generation, felt that *Skipper* would attract the younger set coming up. She did!

New in 1964 was the addition of *Ken's® "Buddy" Allan®*. Very much like other supporting characters on television sitcoms (Remember Maynard G. Crebbs, Dobie Gillis' best friend, or Eddie Haskell, Wally Cleaver's cohort?), *Allan®* was very much like *Midge®*, *Barbie's® Best Friend*, supportive.

I will resist the temptation to sermonize about boys and *Ken* dolls, but let us say that the number of little boys

who had these dolls as a "buddy" was astounding! Many, like myself, were not overly aggressive creatures portrayed by *G. I. Joe®* and the like, but were average college and high school boys much like *Ken* and *Allan*. Through having these two boys as friends, young boys had excellent role models. *Ken* and *Allan* were the perfect gentlemen, the kind of young men you would want to greet your stern maiden aunt at the Thanksgiving Day table.

New also in 1964 was a sleep-eyed version of *Barbie* which, while an interesting piece of *Barbie* history, was a dismal failure basically because she was homely. The shiny plastic face and ghostly eyes looked more like a robot than a doll. By this time Ruth Handler had given up on not having an identity for the dolls. Children and young adults were not projecting themselves as much onto *Barbie* as she had originally believed, but were looking up to her as someone to strive to become. It is only by trying to be perfect that anyone achieves any level of success at all, and *Barbie* and her friends were doing a wonderful job.

By 1965, *Skipper* had gotten two

*G. I. Joe®* is a registered trademark of Hasbro, Inc.

**Illustration 8.** A brownette *Bendable Leg Midge®* from 1965 wears *Fashion Editor* from 1964, while a cool and calm blonde *American Girl Barbie®* models *Outdoor Art Show* from 1965.

**Illustration 9.** One of the rarest of the Couture Period fashions is this outfit, *International Fair* from 1965. It was the only outfit that had a pleated skirt.

new playmates, *Ricky* and *Skooter*. *Ricky*, especially, was very "Leave It To Beaver" looking and an impish lad of about ten. The real news of the year, however, was the complete remodeling of all the original dolls. *Barbie* was, as were all the dolls, given lifelike bendable legs that gave the doll much more posability. This clever mechanism was concealed in the leg and did not show from the outside. The term "lifelike" did indeed apply, but the feature made the dolls difficult to dress as stockings and slacks would not slide easily over the rubbery vinyl necessary to keep the leg flexible. *Barbie's* face was basically the same, except her makeup became richer and creamier, but her real change was her hair. It was now chin length in a "blunt cut," straight across with bangs. Collectors refer to this style as the "American Girl." By the end of the year, the variations of lip colors matched with hair colors was astonishing. Really, no two dolls looked alike. Two other rare versions were a side-parted pageboy and a side-parted flip hairdo, both shown in the illustrations. These dolls are so rare that they often fetch $700 and up even when out of the box!

I might comment that the pricing of *Barbie* collectibles is the least understood in dolls. These dolls were mass manufactured and, as such, only perfect examples are worth anything today as collectibles. The other dolls, with missing makeup, cut hair and chewed toes, are simply used childrens' toys and have little but sentimental value. The value of a never opened package is about two to three times the value of the same object mint, yet unboxed. *Barbie* was not aimed at the collectors' market and even today, executives at Mattel have trouble understanding adults' interest in the doll. Much of our unopened treasures are the result of overproduction from Mattel and much old store stock has turned up.

The story of *Barbie's* development continues with the introduction of *Color Magic Barbie*. One of the loveliest dolls, her long straight hair could be made other colors. She is a lovely collectible from the Couture Period.

Because of the overlap in dates, there are some surprise dolls from 1966 I am saving for the next article. By the mid 1960s, four young men from Liverpool, simply named "The Beatles," would change for a decade the way we dressed, danced and even thought. We were about to be invaded again by the British for the second time in our history! All this would greatly effect the stately Jacqueline Kennedy image of *Barbie* and put her "face to new face" with MOD! Part III will show you a new "groovy" *Barbie*. The baby boomers were growing up, and so was *Barbie*! □

NOTE: All of the information and illustrations are new and are meant to complement the recently-released book by the author, *Doll Fashion Anthology and Price Guide*, available from Hobby House Press, Inc.

# The *Barbie* Look, Part III:
## The Mod Period (1967 to 1971)

The registered trademarks, the trademarks and the copyrights appearing in italics in this article belong to Mattel, Inc., unless otherwise noted.

This is the third part of a four-part series of articles which will highlight the creation of and chronicle the development of *Barbie®*, the world's most famous doll. The first part of the series appeared in the April 1988 issue of **Doll Reader®**, pages 160 to 166 and the second part appeared in the May 1988 issue of **Doll Reader**, pages 122 to 127.

It has been written that more progress and changes occurred from the turn of this century to the present, than from the dawn of civilization to 1900! Our MODern world is spinning at a dizzy pace, indeed. Mattel, sure of *Barbie's* place and image, suddenly found that teenage customs, morals and tastes were changing as quickly as the rest of society. Having had the best-selling doll in history, they obviously were doing something correct. In the world of the present, however, success could never be complacent. The inventor of the Hula Hoop made a fortune overnight, then dwelt in obscurity for life, having had the famous 15 minutes of fame that Andy Warhol predicted for all of us. It suddenly seemed unfair that something so popular as *Barbie* could be threatened by the new youth movement of the moment!

Familiar faces such as Annette Funicello from the "Mickey Mouse Club," and Shelley Fabares from "The Donna Reed Show," once conservative role models for *Barbie* (their hair styles even being duplicated), suddenly had gone "Mod." The word was an euphemism, for "modern" and signified a person who was "rebelling," either superficially with clothing, or totally, by dropping out of society and living in "communes." *Barbie* suddenly seemed matronly and dated. Her face, drown-

**Illustration 2.** Advertisement from *The Barbie Magazine*, Fall 1967, showing how to get your new *Twist 'N' Turn Barbie*. (The bathing suit is an exact copy of the one made famous by Annette Funicello in her "beach party" type movies!)

**Illustration 3.** This new more youthful *Barbie* doll had rooted eyelashes, swinging long straight hair and reflected the youth of the late 1960s. Here dolls model 1967 outfits *All That Jazz* and *Scene Stealers*.

**OPPOSITE PAGE: Illustration 1.** A stunning MOD *Barbie®* arrived in 1967. The epitome of MODern, she was completely redesigned. Here *Barbie* models *Zokko* from 1967 against period wallpaper!

**LEFT: Illustration 4.** The popular miniskirt, made famous by Mary Quant in 1965, was a popular theme of the Mod Period fashions. Here is *Snug Fuzz* from 1967. It featured silver glitter stockings and silver boots. **CENTER: Illustration 5.** Another invention of this period was *Talking Barbie*. A pull ring on her back activated several well-thought phrases that showed *Barbie's* personality. The ponytail was hand-tied at the factory. The fashion is 1967 *Jump Into Lace*. **RIGHT: Illustration 6.** An extra head with hairpieces could be purchased. This *Hair Fair Barbie* has groovy short hair and models *Swirly-Cue* from 1967. The earrings, hose and shoes are much harder to find today than the dress.

ing in sophisticated makeup, was not that of youth. To the casual observer, *Barbie* could have easily been 35 or 40 years old! Her clothing was geared to "proper" attire that one of good breeding would wear at college functions; her idea of "rebellion" would be to not do her homework one night and go to the movies.

One must remember that the baby boomers were now quite restless. Most of the "Leave it to Beaver" dreams that had been promised had not come true. Told that they should do the right thing and they would be rewarded, some, if not most, found that not to be the case. Many times individuals graduating from college found no jobs available. The Vietnam conflict had escalated to catastrophic proportions, and suddenly the most spoiled group of children in history found that things were not what they seemed. Thus was born the term "establishment" to signify the adults, and "Mod" to designate the young and restless!

In 1967, Mattel tried another of the many successful maneuvers that had

kept *Barbie* alive. A "trade-in" program was announced. For $1.50 and your old *Barbie* doll, you could receive a NEW *Barbie*. Mattel not only wanted to update the current doll, but wanted to take steps to assure that the past was forever forgotten. Like Loretta Young, who reportedly bought all her old films so that she could never be seen in outdated makeup, hair styles or clothing, Mattel wanted to erase forever the old image of *Barbie*. The new *Barbie* had a slimmer youthful face, rooted eyelashes and long straight hair. More important, for really the first time in her history, she looked young. (As the boom children aged this would be abandoned, for today's *Barbie*, like Loretta Young, is timeless and ageless and proud of it!) Old dolls were turned in by the millions. It is amazing today how many dolls are left, which is only explained by the fact that over six million *Barbie* dolls were produced annually by Mattel in the early 1960s. If only a small percentage survived, it would still be a staggering number.

Also updated was *Barbie's* ward-

**Illustration 7.** By 1968, the *Twist 'N' Turn Barbie* came in this shrinkwrapped box. In 1969, *Barbie* got another hair style, the "flip" made famous by Marlo Thomas on "That Girl," a popular television series of the period.

**LEFT: Illustration 8.** A mint *Talking Barbie* from 1968 models *Little Bow Pink* from 1968. Many collectors prefer their dolls and clothing out of the package to be viewed in three dimensions. **CENTER: Illustration 9.** After a year of "draft dodging" in 1968, *Ken* was back, completely redesigned in 1969. He was huskier and sported an Edwardian hair style. He looked like many of the soap opera stars of the period such as those on "Dark Shadows," a Victorian horror soap on ABC from 1966 to 1971. **RIGHT: Illustration 10.** "Licensed Friends" was a concept developed by Mattel during the Mod Period. This unusual doll is a standard *Truly Scumptious* from the movie *Chitty Chitty Bang Bang*. She uses the *Francie* head mold and the *Barbie* body.

**Illustration 11.** During this period the "Gift Set" idea continued. Made for stores like Sears, they featured a regular doll with a special outfit. Often the packaging is as interesting as the set as can be seen here in this great Sears *Talking Barbie Gift Set* from around 1967.

robe. The miniskirt, designed by Mary Quant in 1965, was THE symbol of rebellion. Like hair length to men, it became a symbol of independence. If you were part of the Brooks Brothers type of "establishment," you could not wear a miniskirt to work, or sport shoulder-length hair over your necktie. These two things represented the fact that you were free. (Ironically, many of the boom children were still students and were "rebelling" while being supported by parents, which is an easy road to take.)

Mattel had issued *Barbie's Cousin, Francie* in 1965 and she had been a smash hit! Their doll *Twiggy*, the Mod Model, had also been a success. With *Barbie* updated by a new face and new wardrobe, the future was somewhat secure. The problem is, in the fast-paced world of teenage fads, "secure" could mean six months or less. How much simpler life was for *Barbie* when her famous *Enchanted Evening* long pink gown had been designed in 1949 by Castillo (and still looked smashing 13 years later). Those days seemed

gone forever. Fashion once moved by years! To keep *Barbie* current meant a great deal of work because the line for the current year is actually designed perhaps two years before. In a time when hair and shirt length changed more quickly than the weather, this was a major feat!

By the late 1960s, the escalating and unpopular Vietnam conflict had begun to take its toll on youth. Boys really had three choices; enlist, go to college for a coveted II-S deferment or go to Canada. In fact, the "war" so provoked controversy that *Ken, Barbie's* boyfriend was given a year's absence from the line in 1968. It was just too difficult to explain what his political views were! Newscasters, however, STILL commented on what *Ken's* position on Vietnam was, and many speculated that his absence signified he had gone to Canada! Even a doll was not safe from the controversy. In my opinion, this unpopular conflict, which often divided brothers in the same family much like the Civil War, spelled an end to MOD!

By the late part of the year 1970, hemlines were down and a kind of "passive" mood hit youth. Many were burned out from "causes." Others were burned out from drugs that also were becoming alarmingly popular. *Barbie* took a safe approach by adopting "Prairie" looks and back-to-nature lifestyles that were not so conspicuous. Bell bottoms and psychedelic prints were coming on strong. Television shows like Rowan and Martin's "Laugh-In," featured harmless light comedy and zany antics. The seeds were sewn for a simpler life for the next few years. years.

One must remember that glamour was synonymous with frivolity and in a war mentality, that did not seem appropriate. *Barbie* was issued with a suntan and called *Malibu*. This seemed a safe maneuver which would avoid controversy.

Also, *Barbie* was a leader in civil rights, a trend which continues today. Blacks were angry, and rightfully so, at being denied full citizenship in a country which they were asked to defend. Just a short decade earlier, southern states had separate drinking fountains and restrooms for blacks and whites. *Barbie* was again at the forefront of newscasters' snide comments with the issue of *Christie, Barbie's* black girlfriend, in 1968. Ads showed the girls together, attending college functions and having fun. *Barbie* was "mainstreaming," a term which means that she was not segregated. It was a brilliant statement and one which gained Mattel much free publicity. One has to remember that prejudice against anything is a learned trait, and children did not see anything strange in *Barbie* having a black girlfriend.

Many readers of this series of articles will be surprised that a simple child's toy like *Barbie* represented so much. Some will see *Barbie* as they have never seen her before. As someone who lived through all that *Barbie* did, I feel that the fascination to most collectors of *Barbie* other than the fashions and the study of clothing is the brilliant textbook statement she makes about the three decades that she has been "alive." There is no other collectible in history that tells the story of a nation, its struggles, its fads, its glories, better than *Barbie*! Better than a textbook, *Barbie* shows a three-dimensional view of youth in person as it was. Many collectors of *Barbie* chuckle to themselves silently when their critics say that the doll is just a hunk of plastic and not a fine antique. *Barbie* tells the story of MY generation to all who will take the time to get to know her. Much more than a doll, *Barbie* is a phenomenon which, like Shirley Temple, comes along only once! □

**LEFT: Illustration 12.** This period saw the last of the couture outfits. Here a brunette *Hair Fair Barbie* models *Floating Gardens* from 1966 to 1967. By the next year, outfits like this would be considered "out" and matronly. **RIGHT: Illustration 13.** Even the James Bond influence could be seen in *Barbie's* wardrobe such as this sexy and shiny outfit called *Intrigue* from 1967. The stunning doll is a 1969 beauty.

Note: All of the information and illustrations are new and are meant to complement the recently-released book by the author, *Doll Fashion Anthology and Price Guide*, available from Hobby House Press, Inc.

**ABOVE: Illustration 14.** The mini-coat shown here is *Lamb 'N Leather* from 1970. Sheared lambswool coats were a big fashion item of the late 1960s. **ABOVE RIGHT: Illustration 15.** A rare *Twist 'N' Turn Francie, Barbie's MODern Cousin* from 1970 with a rare "no bangs" flip hair style. Dolls such as this are mirrors of our culture in three dimension. **RIGHT: Illustration 16.** The *Barbie* look for the period — long straight hair and young fun fashion such as *Sea Worthy* from 1968, shown here. *Barbie* is barely recognizable from the personality she projected in 1959!

# The *Barbie* Look, Part IV:
## 1970 to 1988

This is the fourth and last part of the series of articles which highlight the creation of and chronicle the development of *Barbie*®, the world's most famous doll. The first part of the series appeared in the April 1988 issue of **Doll Reader**®, pages 160 to 166, the second part appeared in the May 1988 issue of **Doll Reader**, pages 122 to 127 and the third part appeared in the June/July 1988 issue of **Doll Reader**, pages 150 to 155.

The crazy MOD days of the late 1960s were winding down. Like the Hula Hoop, trendy fads disappear quickly. The Vietnam conflict had turned off many teenagers so much that a new word was used to describe this generation: APATHETIC. A person with apathy was someone who just did not care or think about the issues of the day. The use of hallucinogenic drugs, namely LSD, even spawned another new word: PSYCHEDELIC. This word referred to the big splashes of color that were associated with the use of these drugs. The word spilled over in common use to denote anything colorful, such as "flower-power" prints or paisley. (Flower children were the "hippies" or drop outs of the day.)

All this social change happening so rapidly spelled real trouble for Mattel. When *Barbie*® debuted in 1959, change came slower. Now overnight society was acquiring new directions. Some were harmful, some were wonderful, but ALL were happening very rapidly. In the doll industry, the line for a current year must be designed, planned and manufactured often two years in advance. With teenagers changing styles so rapidly, it made "predicting" the direction *Barbie* should go in very difficult.

The first major doll to reflect the 1970s mood of psychedelic apathy was *Live Action Barbie*®. Issued in 1971, the doll sported a "tie-dye" outfit that one could wear to Woodstock, and her usually glamorous hair was simply parted in the middle and held in place with a suede headband. Heavy fringe, another fashion favorite, added to the music image. Like a character from "Laugh-in," a popular television show of the period, *Barbie* and her friends

*Illustration 2. Is that really Ken®? Musicals such as "Jesus Christ, Superstar," gave teens arguments in favor of long hair and beards. Dolls such as this* Now Look Ken® *from the mid 1970s show us as we were.*

*Illustration 3. By the mid 1980s, Barbie® would be a busy executive complete with an attache case and gold credit cards. Her dog, Prince®, accompanies her.*

**OPPOSITE PAGE: Illustration 1.** Live Action Barbie® *from 1971. Shown photographed against a notebook cover used by the author in 1969, the "psychedelic" Barbie® reflects all the trends of the period.*

*ABOVE LEFT: Illustration 4.* *An early 1970s* Living Barbie® *and* Skipper® *show the last of the miniskirts which would return in 1987, and the end of the MOD days of fun, groovy clothing and makeup.* *ABOVE RIGHT: Illustration 5.* *Barbie's® MODern Cousin,* Francie® *was not needed in the 1970s as the MOD days were over. Her quality declined until she was finally discontinued. Here is a* Casey® *and* Francie® *in the mid 1970s, never to be seen again. Collectors want Mattel to reissue* Francie® *as she would be perfect again in today's clothing!* *BELOW Illustration 6.* *Malibu* Barbie® *and* Skipper® *wearing matching outfits like they did in 1964, only this time the dolls reflect the "natural" look Here* Barbie® *looks like model Cheryl Tiegs, the "clean makeup" face of the mid 1970s.*

mirrored the dress code of the underground. These dolls are a great addition to a fashion collection!

By the mid 1970s, America was just plain boring. The baby boomers were tiring of "causes." Many did not even bother registering to vote, as it seemed as if they had no control over events which were shaping their destiny. Calling "time out," some simply dropped out and lived in "communes" or fled to Haight-Ashbury, to sleep out the period.

It was during this time that Mattel had its growth problems. A disastrous fire destroyed the Mexico factory, long a principal manufacturing plant. The Handlers, the terrific couple who had founded Mattel, left management and ownership. The company had grown so fast and undergone so many changes that it was difficult to manage. Under new leadership, Mattel hoped to regain the name for quality they once had.

Fortunately for Mattel, the 16th birthday of the *Barbie* doll was due to arrive in 1975. Eager to use this for publicity, the decision was made to use 1958, the year *Barbie* was trademarked, as her official "birthday." Sensing the wire services would give Mattel a much

needed free "shot in the arm," *Barbie's* 16th birthday arrived with all the fanfare Mattel anticipated.

The doll made for this occasion was a mere shadow of the quality that *Barbie* once was. In many ways so was this generation of children interested in her. Today's parent, not quite the Donna Reed perfectionist for child rearing, seemed content with much less quality. The *Sweet 16 Barbie®*, in all fairness, did not seem as glamorous as her predecessors, not only because of the quality gap, but teens themselves were wearing less makeup and had either long straight hair, or the new "shag" haircut, made popular for both boys and girls by David Cassidy. Trend setting teens such as Maureen McCormick, (Marsha on "The Brady Bunch") and Susan Dey, (Laurie on "The Partridge Family") were the new "girl next door" types.

Another brilliant move which got Mattel back on its feet was its involvement with the 1975 United States Olympics. America was starting to wake up, fortunately. The communes, the drugs, the apathy, were all dying out. Too young to just lay down and let life pass them by, the boom children were waking up and were ready to party. Mattel poured a desperate two million dollars to tie *Barbie* into the Olympic games. Even the dolls made for foreign markets such as Australia, featured *Barbie* as an Olympic athlete with the appropriate gold medal from each country. (*Barbie* in Australia featured a kangaroo on the medal, while Canadian *Barbie* displayed the famous maple leaf!) The themes and the packaging of the dolls were of higher quality than the product itself in many instances, making the mint-in-box items from this period especially valuable. Mattel packaging has always told the story of fads, fashions and pop culture as well as the doll. In these lean years, the packaging was especially important, for it made up many times for the quality gap.

In the late 1970s, the Disco craze hit the United States. Young adults as well as teens suddenly found the beat irresistible. Originally started as a Latin cultural fad, the music spread quickly to other minority clubs. Overnight stars such as Donna Summer, Gloria Gaynor and Vicki Sue Robinson were "turning the beat around." All this

dancing, of course, meant going out. Fashion designers, eager to get America out of Army-Navy store fashions and blue jeans (sometimes frayed to within a hair of falling apart) created swingy flashy styles for men such as wide collar shirts in "Quiana Jersey," the new "in" fabric, and "Danskin" twirling wrap skirts for girls.

At the same time, a classic beauty, Farrah Fawcett-Majors, was becoming a cult figure due to her role as the glamorous Jill Monroe on the hit television show "Charlie's Angels." Her flipped-back layered mane of hair would show up on every teenage girl from Bayonne to Seattle. In some neighborhoods the entire teen populace looked like a Farrah look-alike contest!

Mattel, now more financially solvent after the successful Olympic promotion, issued *Superstar Barbie*®, the most glamorous doll since 1970! Released in 1977, this new doll featured a toothy smile that bore an uncanny resemblance to Farrah. Even the long sun-streaked blonde hair was reminiscent of the star. *Superstar Barbie*® and *Ken*® reflected the Disco craze perfectly! Collectors of fashion dolls

**ABOVE RIGHT: Illustration 7.** *The Disco craze led to dazzling new dolls in 1977 such as this* Superstar Christie®, Barbie's® *black friend.*
**BELOW RIGHT: Illustration 8.** *The public had to be educated to* Barbie's® *new face. Ambassador Greetings put out several greeting cards featuring the* Superstar Barbie® *doll and her Farrah Fawcett-Majors look.* **BELOW LEFT: Illustration 9.** *Licensed friends were a popular product since* Julia® *appeared ten years earlier. Here are the* Osmonds® — *Donny*®, Jimmy® *and* Marie® — *flashing their toothy grins. They were not "friends" of* Barbie®, *but just wore the same size clothing. They were even carefully placed in the back of the Mattel catalog, far away from the front* Barbie® *section!*

*LEFT: Illustration 10. By 1980, country music was making a comeback after Disco died down. Here is* Western Barbie® *riding* Dallas®, *and carrying a copy of her latest country western album! The doll also could wink. It still sported a Farrah inspired hairdo!* **RIGHT: Illustration 11.** *The* Barbie® *family as seen in this centerfold from the May 1972 issue of* Barbie® Talk Magazine. *Shown are* PJ®, Barbie®, *a rare 1971* Francie® *with no bangs,* Ken®, Brad *and* Christie®.

are most fortunate in that through the dolls, these times can be relived, three-dimensionally or met for the first time, within your collection. This, to me, is the real *Barbie* story, the story of US, as a people; what we loved and cherished, and what even made us happy or sad! The collectors of *Barbie* have 30 years of fashions, fads and fancies at their fingertips!

Like all good things, Disco started to die. As it became more and more evident in the mainstream, the minority clubs moved on. (This author sadly remembers MONTHS of lessons to learn how to touch dance and do those dips and swirls, only to have them die out just as I reached my John Travolta best!)

In the early 1980s, the Village People, one of the leaders of the Disco craze, sang "Are you ready for the 80s, ready for the time of your life?" The 1980s were ushered in as a time of equality. Minorities were demanding to be recognized, the women's movement was in full swing, and the baby boom children were now part of the "Establishment," chasing after status symbols now as "Yuppies" (Young Urban Professionals), forced to trust those over 30 of which they themselves now were a part! Words such as "conspicuous consumer" were coined to denote those who drove BMWs and wore "designer" everything. Symbols such as Ralph Lauren's famous polo player took on almost a religious significance, as the boom children, who once scorned the rich, now scrambled

to become them!

Television shows such as "Dynasty" acquainted us with the ultra-rich and their fascinating lives, and for many, chasing power and money became an obsession. ANXIETY became the new "in" way to feel, much like APATHY had been a decade before.

By the mid 1980s, Mattel was securely on top. *Barbie* had never looked better. New themes, and promotional tie-ins to beauty, along with a media blitz to celebrate her 25th anniversary, all gave *Barbie* new status.

All this attention on the new dolls made people wonder about the OLD dolls, and suddenly *Barbie* became the "in" thing to collect. Mattel has responded to this brilliantly, as they always have, and embraced the col-

*LEFT: Illustration 12. This author firmly believes in having FUN with your collection. Here I have made my own "Dynasty" family utilizing various year dolls and outfits to create "Krystle," "Blake" and "Alexis."* **RIGHT: Illustration 13.** *An "acid rock" family portrait, 1971.* Christie®, PJ®, Barbie® *and* Ken® *were rock stars long before* Barbie® *and the* Rockers® *in 1986.*

*LEFT: Illustration 14. Today* Barbie® *and her friends are once again rock stars! Highly creative and imaginative, they are not for every child but the collectors love them. Shown are the fantastic* Billy Boy Barbie® *made for the United States as a 1987 department store special, newly designed* Rocker Ken® *with rooted hair,* Barbie® *looking fresh and pretty as ever, and* Derek®, *the newest man in* Barbie's® *band (and maybe even her life). RIGHT: Illustration 15. Absent since 1967,* Barbie's® *Best Friend* Midge® *has made a stunning comeback in 1988. Looking like she did 21 years before, she still has red hair and freckles! Shown with* California Barbie®, Midge® *will again play a supporting role in* Barbie's® *adventures. The* Beach Boys *have recorded a special record that is packed with* California Barbie®. *Like Annette and Frankie,* Barbie® *is timeless.*

lector with limited edition porcelain dolls, and a line of higher priced fashions that seemed aimed at just them. The introduction of *International Barbies®* take the collectors around the world, for now *Barbie* can be bought domestically in the ethnic guise of all who worship her!

In 1986, *Barbie* again became a rock star, only this time instead of "acid rock" and "psychedelic," her lyrics are light and fluffy, yet with an upbeat image that "We Girls Can Do Anything," which is the logo of *Barbie* in the late 1980s.

It looks like the *Barbie* saga will go on forever. For 1988, the line looks better than ever with the reintroduction of *Barbie's® Best Friend, Midge®*, absent since 1967 and aging well!

For years I have tried to defend, explain or just communicate to mystified friends and family why I have collected *Barbie* since I was a child. My collection reflects allowances spent, vacations denied, yet my collection is in reality, my scrapbook of my life. When I look at my collection of *Barbie* and *Ken*, I see the things I was, the things I was not, and even the type of person I want to be in the future. To *Barbie* collectors worldwide, *Barbie* is the thread of continuity in their lives.

If this series of articles has made you see *Barbie* for the best friend she has been to me, then I have succeeded.

To some, *Barbie* is a social statement, a fashion mannequin, a role model. To me, she is all three, plus a friend of 29 years! I cannot top that one, can you? □

Note: All of the information and Illustrations are new and are meant to complement the recently-released book by the author, *Doll Fashion Anthology and Price Guide*, available from Hobby House Press, Inc.

*LEFT: Illustration 16. The entire* California *line of dolls for 1988, featuring the return of* Christie®, Barbie's® *black friend. Included in this wonderful grouping is a surf shop and a clever hot dog stand! RIGHT: Illustration 17. Mattel is STILL making special dolls that the collector would do well to stash away. Shown here on the left is* Skating Star Barbie® *available only in Canada for the 1988 Calgary Olympics and on the right is* Pink Jubilee®, *a stunning doll for Wal-Mart's 25th anniversary. The prudent collector always is on the lookout for these special issues!*

**Illustration 1.** *A splendid red-lipped 1965 Bendable Leg Barbie® takes to the skies in the rare Pan American Airways Stewardess uniform. This ensemble was only available in 1966 and is considered one of the rarest outfits ever made for Barbie®. Doll,* Dick Tahsin Collection; *outfit,* courtesy of Michael Brown.

# Flying High With *Barbies*

Over the years since the introduction of the *Barbie*® doll in 1959, *Barbie* has been criticized by many (unjustly, in my opinion) as being materialistic, and setting an example of what today we call "conspicuous consumerism." Those of us who have collected and loved *Barbie* since "the good old days" know that this charge simply is not true.

*Barbie* has held more jobs than an entire senior high school class put together, and over the years had many careers (starting with being a top fashion model) that have justified the enormous sums of money she seems to spend on clothes, furniture, cars and other symbols of success. Unlike other dolls or even many people, for that matter, *Barbie* has earned every dime she has made, and in my opinion, can spend it any way she chooses.

Also, as any *Barbie* fan knows, *Barbie* has a heart of gold and shares her wealth with not only her friends, but various charitable activities as storybooks about her have aptly described over the years.

Yes, *Barbie* truly can do anything as her motto tells us. Perhaps one of the most alluring careers *Barbie* has had over the years is that of an airline stewardess.

Originally in 1961, career options for *Barbie* were not as varied as they are today. Instead of a doctor's uniform, *Barbie's* wardrobe consisted of a nurse's outfit for the women's movement was just beginning to break. Her first stewardess outfit, *American Airlines Stewardess*, mirrored one of the few career options open to women. Even in those days, however, discrimination still played a part, for there were physical requirements for the job (in other words one had to be beautiful to serve coffee in an airplane) that today are fortunately ruled out of line for the job. Nonetheless, *Barbie* began her airline career in earnest, and remained active in the stewardess business well into the 1970s, working for not only American Airlines, but Pan American, Braniff

***Illustration 2.*** *A number four brunette* Barbie® *in American Airlines Stewardess, a uniform that debuted in 1961 and was available through 1964.*

*Illustration 3. A close-up of the Braniff Welcome Aboard suit, shown on a Barbie® Hair Fair head.*

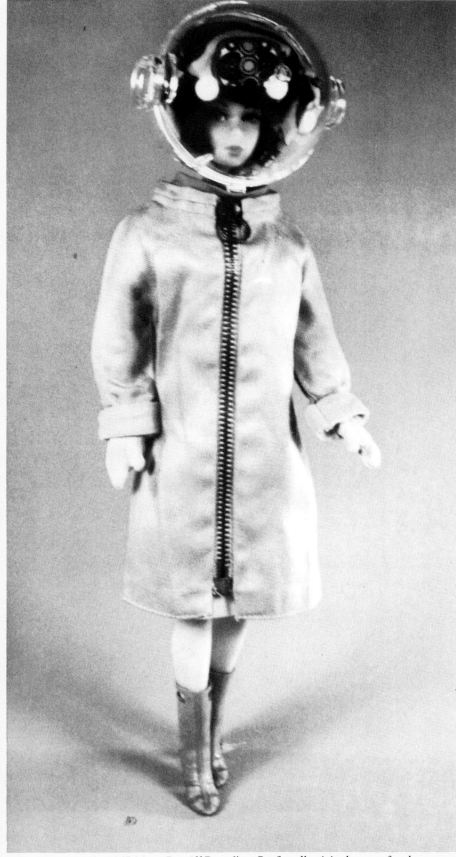

**Illustration 4.** *The 1967 Marx Braniff* Boarding Outfit, *all original except for the replaced bubble helmet. Note the wild go-go boots and oversized zipper which showed the "mod" influence.*

**Illustration 5.** *A brunette* Barbie® Hair Fair *head showcases the velveteen print scarf-hat designed by Emilio Pucci.*

**Illustration 6.** *The* Welcome Aboard *suit, part of the Marx Braniff series, all original except for replaced shoes.*

and later on, United! Yes, *Barbie* certainly flew the globe for the finest, but more importantly, she showed little girls that there were choices in life.

*Barbie's* boyfriend, *Ken®*, accompanied *Barbie* in the early 1960s when she worked for American Airlines, for he was an accomplished pilot. He again joined her in the 1970s when they both worked for United Airlines. True romance in the air!

Kidding aside, these outfits constitute some of the rarest and most desirable outfits ever made for *Barbie*. Many collectors consider the outfit *Pan American Airways Stewardess*, made only for one year (1966), as the most difficult outfit to locate of the 1600 stock

**Illustration 8.** *The* A-Line Hostess Dress *of the Braniff series.*

**Illustration 9.** *The 1974 Mattel catalog showcasing number 7707,* Pilot Uniform, *known as the United pilot uniform.*

**Illustration 7.** *The Braniff* Cocktail Hour *hostess suit which consisted of blue stretch harem pants and turtleneck.*

40

numbered outfits of the mid 1960s. It is not unusual to find a $500 price tag on this outfit whether in or out of the box!

In 1967, a still controversial series of outfits were made for *Barbie* (and for *Barbie* size dolls) by the Marx company, and sold exclusively through Montgomery Ward and the airline. While not having a Mattel label (and available in a gift set with a cheap plastic *Barbie* type doll) the advertising did tie the set in to *Barbie*, and reflected the neon colored uniforms and airplanes that Braniff first showed at the New York World's Fair in 1965. Designed (or at least approved) by Emilio Pucci, the leading Italian designer of the futuristic, these outfits included a plastic space bubble to protect the teased and sprayed hairdos of the day from a windy day at the terminal. Complete with go-go boots, these outfits do reflect the beginnings of the "mod" movement going mainstream that would later be reflected by having Twiggy, the London model, on the cover of *Vogue* magazine. These outfits also have a value of almost $500 each, sometimes more when extra mint or in original packaging.

Finally, by the mid 1970s, *Barbie*

**Illustration 10.** *Page from the 1974 Mattel catalog showing* Barbie's® Friendship. *A realistic United Airlines jet interior was available for realistic play with the uniform outfits.*

and *Ken*, after a hectic stint on United's "Friendship" planes (a smaller airplane was available in *Barbie* size), retired and came down to earth not to leave again until *Barbie* became a woman astronaut in the 1980s!

Yes, over the years, *Barbie* has certainly earned her money AND her wings. Many things can be said about the *Barbie* doll, but "lazy" is certainly not a word that can describe a girl who exemplifies the company slogan: "We girls can do anything, right, *Barbie*?" Right indeed! □

**Illustration 11.** *Original Mattel catalog page from 1975 showing number 7703* Stewardess, *referred to as the United Airlines uniform. This was first shown in 1973.*

Barbie® and Ken® are registered trademarks of Mattel, Inc.

**Illustration 12.** Barbie® *and* Ken® *bid "adieu," taking to the skies in* Barbie's® Sport Plane *that was offered by Irwin Plastics only in 1964.* Ken® *wears* American Airlines Pilot. *This plane is one of the rarest accessory items available for collectors to track down.*

Illustration 1. Number one *Barbie* from 1959 modeling "Wedding Day Set," number 972.

# Goin' to the Chapel with Barbie...

*"Bells will ring, the sun will shine...
I'll be his and he'll be mine..."*
(Early 1960s song
by The Dixie Cups)

Every day our lives are touched by new technology that often makes our heads spin! Familiar things in our homes such as our telephones and television sets have become formidable objects, that some fear operating. Even our dolls are not immune! This year at Toy Fair, new models of old favorites can do everything except balance our checkbooks (and sometimes even that!).

*Barbie* collectors have watched their heroine evolve from a shy sensitive down-to-earth girl to an outrageous rock star! Over the years they have seen *Barbie* change roles, (and clothes), from a top fashion model and actress, to a country western singer, and even an astronaut! Many collectors are wondering if *Barbie* will ever settle down. Some feel that her new image is becoming "extreme."

Well, collectors, take heart, for the truth is, in 1959, when *Barbie* was introduced, the best selling outfit in her wardrobe was her lovely and traditional wedding gown. Called "Wedding Day Set," it retailed for $5.00. Over the years, many wedding gowns have been made for *Barbie*, and EACH one was the biggest selling outfit of its year! In fact, last year's gown, even though it had stiff competition from *Barbie's* Oscar de La Renta fashion line, was the biggest seller! Officially, of course, *Barbie* and *Ken* have never been married. Ruth Handler, the creator of *Barbie*, and the recipient of the second annual **Dolls Of The Year** (DOTY) Lifetime Achievement Award, stated to me that *Barbie* was created so that little girls could have CHOICES about their future. If a little girl dreamed of being a nurse, she could dress *Barbie* as a nurse. If the child dreamed of being a bride, there was the bridal gown. (Of course, you could dream of both!)

**Illustration 2.** This number one *Barbie* is most unusual in that she was shipped from Mattel in 1959 for a store display. Her pink display box was not meant to be sold to the public. She was to be removed from this box and put into the store display. Many retailers saved these shipping boxes for selling the doll once it was discontinued. She also has her round stand, with two prongs for her feet, in a special place in the box.

With all the choices *Barbie* had for life-styles, every little girl, (or boy, through *Ken*) could find an identity for the doll that best suited his/her personality. It was a simple concept, yet one which has endured 28 years! *Barbie* was and still is the biggest selling doll of all time. In my opinion, other fashion dolls have had too rigid a theme, and too strong an identity of their own, so that many children, who did not identify with the created personality, felt at odds with this person.

Even celebrity dolls suffer from this "trait." If the collector or child has no mental identification with the celebrity (for instance if you dislike sports, a doll of a sports figure would have little appeal to you), then the desire to own the object is decreased.

Over the years, *Barbie* has remained popular with children and collectors, because every year the line is varied enough that *Barbie* can be all things to everybody. Last year, *Barbie* went tropical, for those who love the beach; went to the moon, for those who adore science; sang in a rock band; wore high fashion designer clothes; AND was a blushing bride. Children are not expected to identify with (and want) all the dolls and all the clothes, but only those which represent the dreams of that child. Collectors for years have "suffered" because of the large line of *Barbie* dolls, and buy the dolls for different reasons! Collecting *Barbie* is a big commitment in terms of space!

I find it wonderfully refreshing in our fast pace society that children still find the wedding gown the most

**ABOVE: Illustration 3.** Interior of the 1963 "*Fashion Queen Barbie* and *Ken* Trousseau Set," seen in **Illustration 11.** Included with this set is a *Fashion Queen Barbie* with molded hair and three wigs and the featured bridal dress is "Bride's Dream."

**LEFT: Illustration 4.** A 1961 bubble cut *Barbie* models "Bride's Dream," number 947. *Dick Tahsin Collection.*

**LEFT: Illustration 6.** A wedding party, circa 1964. Guests are *Allan®*, *Ken's* buddy, *Ken*, a rare red-headed ponytailed *Barbie* from 1961 and *Midge*, *Barbie's* best friend. The wedding accessories are from "*Tracy®* and *Todd®* Wedding Pak," from 1983.

appealing. Being an astronaut or a rock star does not and should not preclude one from having a warm loving and stable relationship. It is evident from sales records and play patterns that children feel the same way. Today's child wants it all...a career AND a mate, and despite all our fears about our fast paced world, *Barbie* is STILL a traditional, positive, yet forward thinking role model for the child of the 1980s!

Collectors will be surprised at the large listing of bridal fashions and accessories available for *Barbie* over the years. The listing was gathered from Mattel catalogs, and I welcome any additional information any collector may have, such as department store specials or other unknowns.

For someone who never married officially, *Barbie* was certainly the best dressed bride in town! The image of *Barbie* means many things to many people. We, as collectors, thank Mattel, and Ruth and Elliot Handler for giving us a doll that either reminds us of our dreams, or helps us remember our realities. □

*Barbie®, Ken®, Skipper®, Midge®, Francie®, Tutti®, Allan®, Tracy®, Todd®, Steffie®* and *Christie®* are registered trademarks of Mattel, Inc.

**Illustration 5.** A bendy leg *Barbie* models "Beautiful Bride," number 1698.

**Illustration 7. A 1987** *"Barbie* **and the** *Rockers"Barbie* **and** *Ken* **still cling to the traditional values as they get married in "Wedding Party," number 7965, from 1986.**

**ABOVE LEFT: Illustration 8.** "Here Comes the Bride," from 1966 to 1967, number 1665, and *Ken* in "Here Comes the Groom," number 1426. *Barbie* is a bendable leg doll as is *Ken.*

**TOP RIGHT: Illustration 9.** Lid to the 1960 "Trousseau Set," number 858. This lid lacks the artwork that would become a trademark on the later *Barbie* boxes. *Sarah Eames Collection.*

**MIDDLE RIGHT: Illustration 10.** The interior of the 1960 "Trousseau Set," seen in **Illustration 9**, showing a number four *Barbie* and several changes of clothing. The gown featured is "Wedding Day Set." *Sarah Eames Collection.*

**BOTTOM RIGHT: Illustration 11.** Lid to "*Fashion Queen Barbie* and *Ken* Trousseau Set," number 864 from 1963. The cover shows the foundation for the elaborate boxes for Mattel dolls which have been the company's trademark.

**TOP LEFT: Illustration 12.** Lid to the 1964 "*Barbie's* Wedding Party Gift Set," featured high quality art of *Barbie, Ken, Midge* and *Skipper.* By now the identity of *Barbie* was well established. *Sarah Eames Collection.*

**MIDDLE LEFT: Illustration 13.** Interior of the 1964 "*Barbie's* Wedding Party Gift Set," seen in *Illustration 12.* The hair color and style varied for this set. The featured bridal fashion was "Bride's Dream." *Sarah Eames Collection.*

**BOTTOM LEFT: Illustration 14.** 1965 Trousseau Trunk shows the dolls and outfits from the "Wedding Party Gift Set." This trunk is under license and is well made. *Sarah Eames Collection.*

**ABOVE RIGHT: Illustration 15.** By 1966 *Barbie's* wedding was attended by **Francie**®, her MODern cousin, and her sister, *Tutti*®. This is similar in construction to the earlier trunk. *Dick Tahsin Collection.*

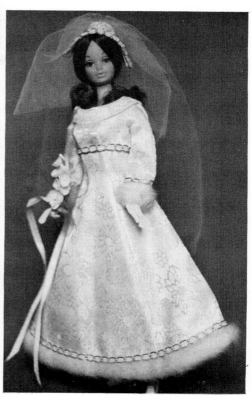

**stration 16.** A *Twist and Turn Barbie* from 7 models "Wedding Wonder," number 1899, n 1968 to 1969. The veil is not original.

**Illustration 17.** A 1969 *Barbie* models "Winter Wedding," number 1880, from 1969 to 1970. The feature of this gown was the real rabbit fur for trim! *Dick Tahsin Collection.*

**Illustration 18.** *Walk Lively Steffie®* models "Bridal Brocade," number 3417, from 1971 to 1972. *Sarah Eames Collection.*

**tration 21.** *Christie®*, *Barbie's* friend, models t Buy Fashion" number 8623 from 1973. ing this period, quality was very poor pared to earlier fashions. By 1976 the origi-styling had returned. *Sarah Eames Col-on.*

**Illustration 20.** This outfit, "Sweetheart Satin" (with no stock number) from 1972, is unusual in that it was a "budget" fashion and one of three bridal gowns available that year. *Sarah Eames Collection.*

**Illustration 19.** A 1970 *Barbie* models "Satin N Shine," number 3493, from 1972.

**A Time Capsule of *Barbie* Wedding Fashions...WEDDING GIFT SETS...**(defined as containing at least one doll and clothing):

1960 "Trousseau Set," #858.
1963 "*Fashion Queen Barbie* and *Ken* Trousseau Set," #864.
1964 "*Barbie's* Wedding Party Gift Set," #1017 (contains *Barbie*, *Ken*, *Midge*® and *Skipper*®).

**TRUNKS**...(defined as cases to hold dolls and clothing):

1965 Trousseau Trunk (with *Midge* and *Skipper* on case).
1966 Trousseau Trunk (with *Francie*® and *Tutti*® on case).

**GOWNS:**

1959 to
1962 Wedding Day Set #972.
1963 to
1965 Bride's Dream #947.
1966 to Here Comes the Bride #1665
1967 (hard to find).
1967 Beautiful Bride #1698 (hard to find)
1968 to
1969 Wedding Wonder #1899.
1969 to
1970 Winter Wedding #1880.
1971 to
1972 Bridal Brocade #3417.
1972 Satin N Shine (Fashion Original) #3493.
1972 Sweetheart Satin (Best Buy, no stock number given).
1973 Best Buy Fashion #8623 (gown unnamed).
1974 to Lovely Bride in Lacey White
1975 #7839 (Get Up and Go Fashion).
1976 to Satiny Sweet Spring Bride
1977 #7176 (Get Up and Go Fashion).
1978 to Bride in White, A Lovely
1979 Sight #2300.
1979 Wedding Belle #2965 (two variations available, Designer Original).
1980 to
1982 Here Comes the Bride #1416.
1983 to
1984 Wedding of the Year #5743.
1985 to
1986 Wedding Party #7965.
1987 Romantic Wedding #3102.

This list is only for *Barbie*, and is only those dresses sold separately. For the past several years, matching outfits have been available for *Ken*, a *Barbie* friend for a Bridesmaid, and *Skipper*, *Barbie's* little sister.

Note: The names listed are registered trademarks by Mattel, Inc. for its fashions.

**Illustration 22.** Variously dressed boxed *Barbies*. The one on the left was made for the European market in the early 1980s. The one in the center is a United States department store special with rooted eyelashes and is very rare today, circa 1977. The one on the right is another department store special from the late 1970s.

**Illustration 23.** *Barbie's* friend, *Tracy*, from the mid 1980s came only as a bride.

Credits and Acknowledgments: I would like to thank Bob Eames for photographing Sarah Eames' dolls, Sarah Eames for the use of her dolls and for the help in researching the listings, Bob Gantz for assistance in the photographing of dolls from the Dick Tahsin collection and to Dick Tahsin for the use of his dolls.

# *"DOLLS LIKE GIRLS"* —
# The Evolution of KATIE, a Living Portrait

Inside all of us is a child...that person who, like Peter Pan, wants to remain young and carefree forever. For most of us, the part of our personality that refuses to accept responsibility, or make decisions, can be satisfied by our interest in dolls. Through collecting, we can recapture, (or capture for the first time), the mystery; the longing of childhood. As we become adults and earn our way, our hobby can be a fullfilling mode of expression for the days of hot summers, ice cream cones, and Christmas mornings.

Doll making has gone through many transitions since the 1930s. An artist named Dewees Cochran, made the individual sculpting of portrait dolls famous. Miss Cochran believed that the face on a doll was the entire message. She became famous designing faces of real live children that could be translated into doll form. Her "Portrait Doll" series, manufactured by Effanbee for B. Altman's and other New York stores, focused on the child as an artistic form in itself, concentrating on the face.

In 1939, this concept was widely accepted by the public. *Life* magazine ran a cover story on Miss Cochran and her dolls. Ads in the *New York Times* focused on the "Portrait Dolls" concept, and made the face the interesting part of its construction. Miss Cochran, putting different heads on stock bodies, with standard wigs and clothing, was creating a whole genre of dolls through the use of faces to make a statement.

Eventually the focus of our nation changed as World War II occupied our minds. Doll companies were lucky to survive, let alone create new ideas. Shortages were commonplace, as industries struggled to provide America's children with the necessities of life, let alone toys.

It was these shortages, and the war,

**Illustration 1.** *Life's* Cover Story, April 3, 1939, featured the "Portrait Dolls" of Dewees Cochran.

that changed the "face" of the doll industry. Companies began to make compromises to stay in business. It became increasingly commonplace to use the same standard mold over and over to create new characters. Through the use of wigs and clothing, a new persona could be invented. At first this concept was executed in the style typical of war shortages. Effanbee, the very company responsible for the glamorous "Portrait Dolls" of Dewees Cochran, started to issue those very same dolls with one standard face, referred to today as the "Little Lady"

face. As the war and our nations problems deepened, materials such as human hair became luxuries; substitutions such as yarn were used. The highly detailed composition bodies gave way to cloth; clothing was constructed as cheaply as possible. Today, the collector views these dolls as an imaginative response to a time of need, yet to a nation used to the luxury brought forth by the doll industry they must have seemed adequate at best.

Madame Alexander and Effanbee evolved this concept, as did other companies, into a standard way of

doing business, and by the early 1950s, most major manufacturers were using the same faces on all their dolls. American Character, Madame Alexander, Mary Hoyer, Arranbee, and Effanbee were all using the standard 14in (35.6cm) or 18in (45.7cm) hard plastic doll (rumored to be made by Allied Plastics of New York). These companies, basically using the same molds, were devoting all their energies to competing through wigs and clothing. In this post-war 1950s period, faces were all but forgotten.

Finally, in another twist of irony, Effanbee again started the trend of portrait sculpting in their "Legends" series, as W. C. Fields revived character dolls that looked like the person intended.

In the early 1980s a company named JESCO recognized that the collector was starting to want more from their dolls than just blank faces. Two sensitive and creative people, Nancy Villasenor, and Jim Skahill, were the brains behind this venture. Jim had been involved in the doll business for many years as a manufacturers representative. He had seen what had sold and what had not, and began to realize that the direction of the doll world was changing.

In a well-meaning, yet misdirected manner in the late 1960s, the U.S. government had become obsessed with the safety of children's toys. Despite

**LEFT: Illustration 2.** The niece of Nancy Villasenor, with Katie ™, her own "portrait doll."
**BELOW LEFT: Illustration 3.** Nancy Villasenor, the creator of Katie ™, and her inspiration.
**BELOW: Illustration 4.** Quality control at Jesco, Inc. is very stringent. Here a worker puts the finishing touches on an outfit.

the fact that no documented cases of children being injured from fine fabrics or accessories could be proven, a witch hunt ensued in which U.S. agents actually went into toy stores and removed earrings and other "dangerous" accessories from dolls never meant to be played with by younger children. Like many other times in our history, the consumer was having his rights taken away. Our quest for "protection" was leading to the downfall of fine American collectibles.

Collectors as a whole were not sympathetic with this movement. JESCO began to hunt around for ideas. Jim Skahill had long seen the quality of European imports such as Italocremona, Furga, CR Club, Zapf and Corelle. Thanks to consumer and collector protests, the government was easing up on ridiculous restrictions. Nancy and Jim had a brilliant idea. Jim had been involved with KEWPIE when Amsco/Milton Bradley was licensed by Joseph Kallus to manufacture his CAMEO dolls. Jim believed that the appeal of KEWPIE was universal.

Nancy arranged a meeting with Joseph Kallus, who was then living in New York. At this meeting, at the Princeton Club, JESCO secured the CAMEO KEWPIE rights, and Jim and Nancy began manufacturing. They exhibited the first line of KEWPIE at the Nurenberg Toy Fair in Germany. People there had never heard of Rose O'Neil or KEWPIE'S antics, yet fell in love with the pudgy face toddler. New ideas began to grow in Nancy's head.

While working on the 1984 line, Nancy began to dream. "My goal seemed to be to manufacture a doll

**Illustration 5.** Each "Katie ™" is hand packed to make sure each doll is a quality collectible.

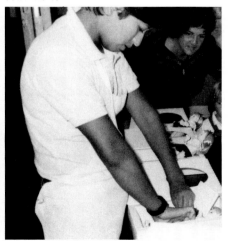

**Illustration 6.** "Katie ™," the perfect portrait of a perfect little girl.

that looked like a child, rather than one which looks like a doll. I took photos of children in parks, schools, or at play. While I felt I was on the right track, nothing seemed to fit quite right."

In many situations one cannot see the "forest for the trees." Nancy had been very close to her 3½ year old niece, and one day realized, while watching her at play, that here was the face she had been looking for. Here was her inspiration.

"As the sculpting took shape, I became more and more inspired. Not only by her physical features, but more so by her captivating spirit and playfullness. I saw how all little girls might be related to Katie; the tilt of her head, the expression she assumed, her cloth-

ing designed to be as all little girls dress — for school, for party or for play. Katie was real and alive for me and I wanted her to be so for the 'little child' for whom she was purchased, whether that 'little child' was 4 or 40!"

Katie was a smash success in 1984. As the real Katie grows up, so will Cameo's Katie. Like the Dewees Cochran "Grow-Up" dolls, Katie will grow up with children and collectors in new editions each year that reflect her new maturity. In the words of Nancy, "I see Katie as I do a montage of treasured family photos. We put our favorites on the wall to delight us with today's precious moments. As we grow, we add the new pictures as they become equally special and an important part of us."

**Illustration 7.** "Katie ™" packaging is made to the same exacting standards as the doll itself. The clothing, sold separately, is attractively packaged. Each doll bears a wrist tag with a cameo, the logo of "Cameo."

**LEFT: Illustration 8.** A doll for all reasons — a child, or collector, "Katie ™" captures the hearts of all.

**Illustration 9.** "Katie Kollectables," the deluxe line for 1985, featuring European wigs and fabrics.

The collector of 20th century dolls is lucky today to be witnessing another evolution in ideas. After so many years of the same faces, a new direction, one inspired from the past, is taking shape. Jesco is one of the companies who recognizes this need in the collector to have a doll created in the image of a child. Like Dewees Cochran before Nancy Villasenor is meeting the challenge of the 1980s with enduring dolls like girls.

(Inside Katie's tag is a poem that describes her perfectly).

Katie's the name of this cute little miss.
Who pouts and throws tantrums then gives you a kiss.
She's spunky and playful; her dresses are frilly
When she romps with her Daddy she can be very silly.
Katie's shy and demure when she's trying to please
But mischievious and spunky and always a tease.
You'll love to raise Katie, your very own doll.
She reminds me of you when you were so small.

**Illustration 10.** New for 1985, "Katie ™" can change fashion looks in this gift set called "Katie Koordinates."

**BELOW: Illustration 11.** "Katie ™ Goes Kollectible." Jesco's new line of an adorable toddler doll comes in various costumes, which are available separately or with the doll.

# YOU!
## ...Boys and Girls Forever:
### Takara Company's Lifelike Children

**Illustration 1.** *The back of the packaging showing all the different school uniforms available. Several face molds were used and there were many different hair styles available.*

**Illustration 2.** *The more recent* You *dolls look more like fashion models. Note the model's poses on the packaging.*

One of the more exciting things to do at Toy Fair in New York, (that ubiquitous place where all things seem magical) is to "walk the halls" and see what the little off-the-mainstream companies are up to!

This author NEVER misses a visit to the fabulous Takara showroom because, for the past several years, this proud Japanese firm (which makes mainly boys' toys for the United States) displays its fantastic doll line that is NOT for the United States market, but for the Japanese. The quiet polite Oriental girl in the showroom never seems to know what the dolls are. It also always surprises me that the press has never picked up on the incredible quality and lifelike features these dolls have.

Perhaps it is out of embarrassment. The Takara Company did once make an American version of its classic *Licca* doll, its best selling doll in Japan. She was called *Lisa* and was almost a cruel joke. The quality was miserable, the hair thin, the fashions cheaply made and there was no catalog. Imagine the surprise I got when an airline steward friend brought me a *Licca* doll from Japan. I could not believe my eyes. The imaginative hair style, the fine fabrics and fully photographed catalog were, well, let us just say it was light-years away from *Lisa*.

That year, 1984 I believe, I went to the Takara showroom with both dolls. I asked the polite and proper Oriental gentleman why? Why the difference in quality? At the answer, it

**Illustration 4.** *A more "American" style* You *doll sports an all-American rugby shirt and long straight hair with bangs.*

**Illustration 5.** *Using a broader face mold with a smile, this* You *doll is wearing another school uniform that almost looks like an American Catholic school uniform.*

58

was I who bowed my head. It seems that the American middle class does not require such quality, and that American children are not taught to cherish their possessions. What a pity, for it did not used to be that way.

Since then, I have watched *Jenny*, another popular Takara doll evolve into a doll like none sold here. One remembers also that in the early to mid 1980s the company manufactured *Barbie®* and re-created a legend with collectibles so real it was uncanny.

In 1987, I visited the Takara showroom and in back of the desk stood two dolls. One, a boy, looked like a Japanese schoolboy, complete with bookbag. The girl, in traditional uniform, almost seemed to be breathing.

Reluctantly I asked if I could examine the dolls closer. In hand, they felt heavy and solid with fully rooted hair and clothing that was completely tailored. I asked about the names and the girl said they had none, but would not be for sale in the United States. They were on exhibit mainly to show the capabilities of the Takara company.

I was seething mad when I left because, once again, Americans would not be getting (nor would they desire, it would seem) a quality doll.

Lest the reader think I am un-American in my views, let me say quite the contrary, for I feel it is shame that dolls like this are not sold here.

At the risk of sounding like my grandfather's "when I was

**Illustration 6.** *One of the* You *doll models, this young lady sports a tailored dress with shoulder bag and spectator shoes. She has a Paulina Porzikova (a popular American model) hair style that features a side-parted long straight hairdo.*

**Illustration 7.** *A "trashy but flashy"* You *doll sports a black vinyl miniskirt with black fishnet knee socks.*

your age" stories, let me remind the readers that not too long ago, fabulous quality dolls by Madame Alexander, American Character, Ideal and others graced the space under the family Christmas tree. A child was given beautiful things and taught to care for them, for replacing them would not be easy.

This attitude, which we have seemed to have lost, is still alive in Europe and Japan, where children are taught a word we have forgotten — respect: respect for others, for our possessions and even ourselves.

The Takara Company dolls are so outstanding that hopefully, enough pressure will be put to bear on them and they will sell their dolls here in the United States!

The dolls I viewed which looked so much like children were larger than *Barbie*, and eluded me for quite awhile. Of course, not knowing their names did not help matters. I had stumped my airline personnel friends.

Finally, one airline buddy of mine brought back the two dolls that were in the Takara showroom. They had no names, because they represented ALL children and thus were part of humanity.

For several weeks I kept this pair unopened on my desk, just staring into their faces, trying to imagine who they were.

I went to the library and researched as best I could, what a school day in Japan was like. It seemed far different from the mall-marching gum-chewing loud and rude children I was used to seeing locally! It seems as if the learning years are full of fun, but the type of fun where one learns such things as dance, music, playing musical instruments, poetry and much philosophy of a culture that goes back thousands of years. Through these dolls, I was learning about a whole different way of life. How sad the children here would be denied that chance to learn through these beautiful dolls.

My bubble of Oriental philosophy and Haiku afternoons broke when I opened the boxes finally and glanced at the brochure that accompanied the dolls.

While the back of the box depicted only school uniforms, the inside was quite a different story. Here the same dolls were shown "Westernized," or at least as seen through the eyes of the Japanese. Trendy miniskirts with ruffled knee socks, jean jackets and satin windbreakers — why some of the outfits looked like the same as those on the mall-marching

gum-chewing loud and rude children I saw daily! Could it be my rose-colored glasses were on again?

The real crushing blow came when another of the school children arrived in a box that showed "Madonna-like" black vinyl miniskirts with fishnet knee socks! My airline friend, the father of two children, snickered at my naive assumptions. It seems as if Japanese children long to be American in some ways (especially dress), and that even McDonald's was doing well in Japan! Could it be that there is room in their culture for the arches in gold of not only the past philosophers, but McDonald's as well? Well, let us hope they can handle it all was my first thought!

Finally the second season of *You* dolls were on display. This time, another image had replaced the school children of Japan look, and the "flashy trashy" look of black fishnet. These dolls, different in face mold and hair style, looked exactly like the top models of the day here. Almost perfect likenesses of Paulina, Kim Alexis and Cindy Crawford stared at me from the package back. The dolls were posed in model stance, complete with the obligatory "run your fingers through your hair" look. The outfits were tailored, miniskirted (but not trampish) and very "rich" looking in fabric. How far these dolls had come in two years!

Finally, my buddy called one day with another surprise: a *You* doll young lady in a traditional Japanese kimono!

My face smiled all by itself as I saw the progress that two short years had made on these wonderful dolls.

This is what doll collecting is all about, I mused as I added this chic traditional lady to the school children and the modeling school! It is learning about the old, adding the new and coming up with the best of both! It is something the Japanese have known for centuries. Look to the past, look to the future, but use the knowledge this gives you for the present.

The *You* dolls did live up to their name. In studying them, I did become them and they became me. It was an exciting adventure!

Readers who want these dolls and other dolls manufactured by the Takara Company sold in the United States should tell their local toy stores about them to see if they can get the dolls. Perhaps someday these lovely dolls can be on our favorite retailer's shelves! □

*Barbie*® is a registered trademark of Mattel, Inc.

***Illustration 8.*** *The inside brochure of the miniskirted doll shows many more American looks including bubble dresses with lacy knee socks and a black leather jacket for the boy.*

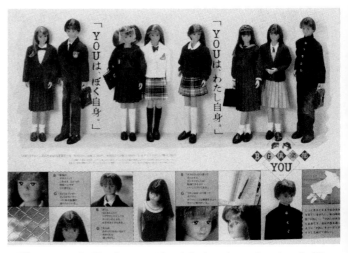

***Illustration 9.*** *The front inside of the brochure showing the* You *dolls. The bottom photographs are the typical "portrait" type photographs that make the Takara dolls seem real.*

**Illustration 10.** *The You dolls represent YOU, the children of all nations. Shown here are two of the most beautiful dolls dressed as Japanese school children.*

# Beautiful or Truly Outrageous,
## Part I

## "It all depends on the mood I'm in"...Jem™

Oriental girl taken in by Jacqui™ when Aja™ was 11 years old, and Shana Elmsferg™, a black girl with many talents. The girls grew up with much love, happiness and times spent with Rio Pacheco™, the cute boy next door.

Emmet Benton™ was a scientist, and for years tried to develop a computer that would link music to 3-D holographic images. Finally, as he neared suc-

*OPPOSITE PAGE: Illustration 1.* Jem™, the rock star doll of the 1980s, and boyfriend, Rio Pacheco™, set the pace in dazzling evening wear. *ABOVE: Illustration 2.* Jem™ is in reality the shy Jerrica Benton™, long time friend and neighbor of Rio™. With the help of her Jemstar earrings, she becomes Jem™. (The poster was available only by mail from Hasbro.) The blank face on Jem™ was rapidly discontinued in 1987.

The world was in love with beautiful Jacqui Benton™. Once famous as a singing sensation, she left her career to marry scientist Emmet Benton™, founder of Starlight Music™, and raise her daughters, Jerrica™ and Kimber™. As a foster girl, she remembered the loneliness, and created Starlight House™, a home for girls without families.

As Jerrica™ and Kimber™ grew up, their lives were touched by many people such as Aja Leith™, the

*Illustration 3.* Emmet Benton™, famous scientist, made a computer, Synergy™, which provides the holograms for Jem™ and her friends.

*cess, he realized that such a machine in the wrong hands could destroy world peace.*

*Jacqui™, eager to resume her famous singing career, planned a comeback, but was tragically killed in a plane crash on her first trip. Shaken by her death, Emmet™ never recovered. He poured all his energies into making his computer a reality. Finally, as he realized his own death due to cancer was imminent, he named his computer Synergy™ (synthetic energy), and hid his creation. His last legacy was a flashing pair of Jemstar earrings to be left to his eldest daughter, Jerrica™ to control Synergy™ and the computer-generated holograms. He wanted to die knowing that his daughters, Starlight Music™ and Starlight House™ would live on, helped and enhanced by his computer creation.*

Glamour, glitter, fashion and fame all combined together equals the most charismatic doll of the 1980s ..*Jem™*! Born from a brilliantly written story, and the popularity of such mega pop stars as Madonna, Belinda Carlisle and Whitney Houston, *Jem™* burst on the scene in the fall of 1986 as the most exciting new doll ever created.

Shown at Toy Fair in 1986, *Jem™* was everything anyone could want in a first-class promotion. By June, the trade papers were touting amazing statistics about her creation. Her new size of 12½in (32cm), and her high quailty, high fashion wardrobe and blinking LED Jemstar earrings gave her a personality right out of a glitzy novel.

Hasbro Inc., the toy company responsible for *Jem™*, announced in *The Licensing Book*, June 1986, that *Jem™* would be introduced simultaneously around the world. Twenty-one licensees with an emphasis on apparel, accessories and personal care items were granted. Maurene Souza, Hasbro's vice-president/marketing for girls' toys states in the above issue: "The marketplace needed a more contemporary fashion doll with a totally different look and appeal."

*Jem™* was introduced through a made-for-television movie, then developed into a weekly half-hour series of well-written beautifully animated almost adult themed shows. The *Jem™* television show combined adventure and fashion with music videos, introduced exactly as done on "MTV," only they were animated. Hasbro scheduled a $10 million advertising campaign for *Jem™* that included highly sophisticated television commercials developed by Charlex, the company that produces award-winning rock videos. The commercials, scheduled for cable as well as regular television, introduced the nation to *Jem™*, the singing sensation of the 1980s! A joint promotion was carried out with "MTV" including doll-size black "MTV" jackets for *Jem™* and *The Holograms™*, her rock band, and a singing contest called *"Jem's™ Truly Outrageous Audition Contest."* Included with each doll were fabulous posters and mail-in offers. Hasbro encouraged the collectibility of the doll, and when *Jem™* hit the stores, everyone was eager with anticipation.

Beautifully coordinated, the promotion included dolls with cassette tapes of professionally recorded songs sung by the doll's character. The songs coordinated to names of stunningly made outfits, and the whole package of doll, song and costume tied into the television show! It was not only truly outrageous, but truly brilliant as well.

At Toy Fair in 1987, as I toured the *Jem™* gallery, I was almost overwhelmed at the new line. *Jem™* had a new smiling

***TOP: Illustration 4.*** *Kimber Benton™, younger sister of Jerrica Benton™, is a songwriter and helps* Jem™ *plan her latest videos and songs at the fabulous* Jem™ *piano that actually works and converts to a water bed!* ***BOTTOM: Illustration 5.*** *Rock 'N Curl* Jem™ *on the* Jem™ Stage™, *leads sister* Kimber™ *and* The Holograms™, Shana™ *and* Aja™.

***Illustration 6.*** *The Starlight House™ foster girls visit* Jem™ *at KJEM,* Jem's™ *radio station. Rio™ ably runs the controls. Each girl leaves with* Jem's™ *latest album!*

**Illustration 7.** The Misfits™, *a competitive rock band which will stop at nothing to destroy* Jem™ *and her world! Top:* Clash™ *and* Jetta™; *bottom:* Roxy™, Pizazz™ *and* Stormer™

face, and the costumes were broadway show quality. Dazzling packaging, up-to-the-minute graphics, sizzling videos and a palette of licensed products made *Jem*™ seem so real. I, like many collectors, caught "*Jem*™ Fever" quickly, and hounded the stores looking for the newly released products.

By fall of 1987, despite the television program often placing number one in children's shows, and the release of *Jem's* television movie on video cassette, it was apparent that the product was just not moving. At Toys R Us, stock piled high to the ceiling. At independent stores such as F.A.O. Schwarz (which earlier in the year devoted an entire corner to *Jem*™ complete with continuous showings of her rock videos), sales were, as one employee commented, "sluggish."

In November, rumor hit that *Jem*™ would be discontinued, and that Hasbro, which surely must have designed a 1988 line by this time, would not be offering *Jem*™ at Toy Fair next year.

I called Wayne Charness, Public Relations Director at Hasbro and was ironically put on hold while the *Jem*™ theme played in the background, and was told that no decision had been made.

The week before Christmas, stores in Philadelphia had marked ALL the *Jem*™ line 50 percent off! While delighted (gleefully filling two entire shopping carts amid stares from other shoppers and employees), I realized that perhaps the most exciting doll to come along since *Barbie*™ debuted in 1959 was going to be discontinued.

At this point, as any good investigative reporter would do, I tried to learn the truth about the demise of *Jem*™. What could have gone wrong with a doll that just a few months earlier was destined to be around for years! Telephone calls to various sources produced dead end after dead end. Finally a lucky break occurred when I was able to connect with a freelance designer who had worked on the *Jem*™ Project. In a

Truly Outrageous!

*Illustration 8. The world of Jem™ was depicted in high quality artwork such as this poster packed with the 1986 dolls.*

**Doll Reader**® exclusive, in two parts, I am going to reconstruct the *Jem*™ story, from start to finish, AND even show you the entire 1988 line that was designed, but never produced! *Jem*™ was destined to be a real star in the true sense of the word!

At Starlight House™, Jerrica Benton™ was having problems. Emmet Benton™ did not know how to manage things, it seemed, and both Starlight House™ and Starlight Music™ were in trouble. A young man who once impressed Benton with his aggressiveness and became co-chief executive of Starlight Music™, had gained too much power during Benton's illness and absences due to working on Synergy™. This young man, Eric Raymond™, was eager to seize control of Starlight™ from the young Jerrica™ and would stop at nothing to accomplish his mission.

Finally the secret of Synergy™ was revealed to Jerrica.™ When she put on the Jemstar earrings, she could project a hologram, or three-dimensional image of herself as Jem™, an up-to-the-minute singing sensation. The Starlight House™ friends, Aja™ and Shana™, found that Synergy™ could create costumes, equipment and settings for them to raise enough money to perform as Jem™ and The Holograms™.

Raymond, undaunted, formed his own company, Misfit Music™ fronted by three low-life type girls, named The Misfits™, whose sole mission in life was to destroy Jem™ and make Jerrica's™ life miserable. One of these girls, Pizazz™ (whose real name was Phyllis Gabor) came from a very wealthy family where her mother had deserted her when she was a child, and her father, short on time, but long on cash,

67

**Illustration 9.** Jem™, *the ultimate fashion doll, gets ready to conquer her world, thanks to the legacy left by her father which makes her a mega-star!*

*had spoiled her rotten, including backing Misfit Music™. The Misfits™ in the television series stop at nothing to sabotage Jem's™ plans. At times, the violence is overwhelming as the girls plow their way through crowds of people, injuring dozens of bystanders, and destroying millions of dollars in property. For some reason they never seem to be punished for their misdeeds, and go on in adventure after adventure wrecking havoc.*

"MTV" (Music Television) premiered August 1, 1981. It was the brainchild of Robert W. Pittman. Only Ted Turner, who introduced "Cable News Network" can be said to have matched Pittman for shaping and reshaping attitudes about television during the 1980s. Pittman claimed the networks never knew how to present music well on television. His idea was to have stars make elaborate videos of their songs and he would play them for a combination of sight and sound. The idea was so simple that *Fortune Magazine* named "MTV" "Product of the Year" in 1981. It was Michael Jackson, with his mega video hits of "Billie Jean" and "Beat It" that in 1983 exemplified the music video scene. By 1985 "MTV" was a household commodity, reaching most cable subscribers, but more importantly, it was making a new era of music with an emphasis on fashion. A design team at Mattel had already put together a way to capitalize on this with a 1986 promotion planned for *Barbie®*, to become a rock star a la Madonna, with a band, *The Rockers®*.

If you think the government guards its secrets, you should see the toy industry! In the highly competitive world of dolls, kingdoms can be made and lost on one leaked idea.

About the same time, the *Jem™* Project, as it was referred to at Hasbro, was being launched. To ask which came first, Mattel or Hasbro, depends on which company you ask. Both, naturally claim first dibs on the idea, but the real point is that both companies planned extensive campaigns centering around rock star dolls. In an interview with Al Corosi, senior vice president for Hasbro, at Toy Fair 1987, Mr. Corosi was eager to share Hasbro's early ideas.

Originally, *Jem™* was to be called "M," for the tie-in to "MTV," but corporate lawyers squelched that when they discovered a letter cannot be copyrighted! The plans had gone so far that plastic guitars had already been made in the shape of an "M" to accompany the doll, so a name with "M" had to be used. Finally, as the story line developed about the Jemstar earrings, the name *Jem™*, evolved. *The Holograms™* were originally conceived in early planning stages to be all male, but that bit the dust when it was learned that *The Rockers®* accompanying *Barbie®* would be female. Finally, the voice of *Jem™* on all her videos, tapes, and television would be kept a secret, to add to the mystery.

In the spring of 1987 after repeated attempts to "snoop" out the voice of *Jem™*, I hit pay dirt! Mary Martin and Carol Channing were appearing at the Forest Theatre in Philadelphia. As I thumbed through *Playbill,* the official theatregoers guide, I was stunned when a credit for Kathy Andrini listed her as the voice of *Jem*™. Miss Andrini is best known for her role on Broadway as "Trixie True...Teen Detective," and was on tour with "Cats," as well as appearing in a "Magnum PI" commercial. I was able to confirm this fact, and a big piece of the puzzle was solved.

In my opinion, it was NOT *Jem*™ and *The Holograms*™ that caused the demise of the *Jem*™ Project, but the utter shameless violence of *The Misfits*™, coupled with their appearance (hardly prep school), that many parents and even children took great exception to.

Newspapers featured articles announcing that toys had gone too far. Parents' groups felt even the *Jem*™ television show was just a half-hour commercial for the dolls. (Actually, the dolls were NEVER advertised on the show.)

At F.A.O. Schwarz, where the videos ran continuously, parents seemed appalled at the immorality and lack of punishment *The Misfits*™ reveled in. As an adult, I found them, well, devilish, but extreme and often laughable. I do concede that role models they were not. Of course, the whole idea was the basic and timeless struggle between good and evil, and while they went unpunished, each episode ended with them steaming mad that they did not get the best of *Jem*™. Each drama was, in a sense, a morality play, but one wonders if many parents or children viewed them as such.

The other contributing factor to the demise of *Jem*™ and one that played a much larger part, was her size. No doll that has not been *Barbie*® size has ever made it beyond the two-year mark. Kenner had tried with *Darci*™, in 1977. (For more information on *Darci*™, see "*Darci*™ Fever" by this author, in the November 1987 **Doll Reader**®, pages 150 to 158.) *Jem*™ was the same size a *Darci*™. In fact, many of the parts could have been made from the same molds, including the stand for the dolls. The design team on the *Jem*™ Project must have looked at *Darci*™, for the two dolls are identical in too many ways for it to be a coincidence! Parents simply view toys differently than collectors do. I was dazzled by *Jem*™ and willingly spent my money for things I will have a lifetime. This is not so with the parent who was being asked to shell out a small fortune for doll clothing that was not interchangeable with dolls already at home. Hasbro was gambling that the doll and the clothing would be so appealing that this would happen. It did not. Unfortunately, another problem for *Jem*™ is that she was caught between a "good" doll like Madame Alexanders, and the discount store dolls. Anything over $9.99 at a chain toy store in a fashion doll is usually passed over. When sold at higher prices at fancy stores, the doll still did not do well because her "discount house" image followed her! To sum it up, the negative image of *The Misfits*™ which spilled over into *Jem*™ and her unusual size, spelled the demise of the most creative and beautifully designed fashion doll in 30 years! □

Coming in Part II: *The Misfits*™ are replaced to "save" the image of *Jem*™, but it was too late! Also, see the entire 1988 line and further details of the life of *Jem*™...the star of the 1980s.

The following are registered trademarks of Hasbro, Inc.: Starlight Music™, Jerrica™, Kimber™, Starlight House™, Aja Leith™, Shana Elmsferg™, Rio Pacheco™, *Synergy*™, *Jem*™, *The Licensing Book*, *The Holograms*™, Jerrica Benton™, Misfit Music™, *The Misfits*™, Pizazz™, Rio™, Rock 'N Curl Jem™, *Jem*™ *Stage*™, Clash™, Jetta™, Roxy™, Stormer™, Emmet Benton™, Jacqui Benton™, Eric Raymond™, *Barbie*™ and *The Rockers*™ are registered trademarks of Mattel, Inc. *Darci*™ is a registered trademark of Kenner Products Corporation.

**Illustration 10.** Jem™, *the truly outrageous singing sensation of the 1980s, greets an eager audience!*

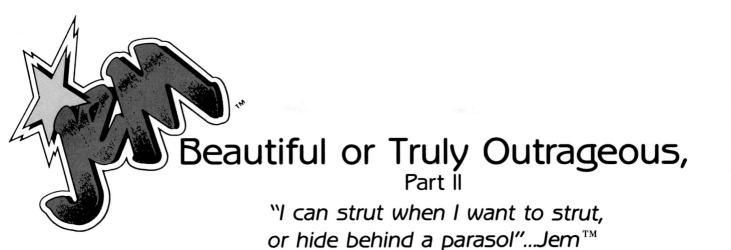

# Beautiful or Truly Outrageous,
## Part II

## "I can strut when I want to strut, or hide behind a parasol"...Jem™

The first part of this article appeared in the April 1989 issue of the **Doll Reader**®, pages 207 to 213.

*Starlight House™, the foster home for girls, had a new home. Jem™ and The Holograms™, in a battle of the rock bands, had won a new mansion. Not pleased, The Misfits™ plotted their revenge.*

*Jem™, meanwhile had had a slight falling-out with Shana™. A new drummer, Raya Carmen Alonso™ joined the group. Shana™ realizes her mistake and returns, remaining active in the group and designing their costumes.*

*The big news for Jem™ is that after a fierce battle with Eric Raymond™, a master tape of Jacqui Benton's™ last songs has been located and Jem™ will have Starlight Music™ release the album as a tribute to her mother.*

The decision to discontinue the Jem™ Project was not made lightly. The people I interviewed who worked on the project said that much, much discussion took place. In an interview in *Toy and Hobby World*, May 1988, Al Corosi, senior vice president of Hasbro, said in restrospect, "We knew little girls liked playing with fashion dolls, and we wanted to make Jem™ a different kind of fashion doll. So we made her a rock and roll star that travels all over the world and maintains a home for orphan girls. But it was a fantasy that was too far out for most girls. It was something they could not identify with; it had no "hook" to reality."

Before the decision to discontinue Jem™ was made, Hasbro, realizing along with Mattel and even "MTV" that the era of the rock video being enough to carry a product was over, HAD decided to try another approach with Jem™...one that would possibly have worked, but now was to be abandoned.

*Everyone knew that Jem™ had stage presence. Kimber Benton™ had a boyfriend, Jeff Wright™, who was a Hollywood stuntman,. He saw potential. Another of Kimber's™ boyfriends, Shawn Harrison™, a British teen idol, wanted to star with Jem™ in a movie. As can only happen in Hollywood, all these forces came together and Jem™ appeared in a B-movie. Her work was so wonderful that she was nominated for an academy award! Producer Howard*

*Sands then cast Jem™ in the blockbuster movie Star-bright after a temperamental actress walked off the set. Jem™ became an overnight sensation. An entire wardrobe of fashions would be needed for her new career. Jem™ was going Hollywood! She would soon be an oscar winner and known in the trade as Holly-wood Jem™!*

The *Jem™* Project designers envisioned a new promotion with *Jem™* as an actress. Thinking this more a "hook" on reality, the *Hollywood Jem™ Fashions™* would be designed. They would be introduced slowly on the animated series, much the same way the *Glitter 'N Gold™* fashions were. A cassette tape would come with *Hollywood Jem™* featuring her new theme song. The campaign would feature the slogan, "There she is, on the boulevard, *Hollywood Jem™*!" Another new character was to be introduced in doll form, *Regine Cezare™*. Made from the same mold as *Raya™*, *Regine™* would be from Martinique, and would become the official costume designer of *Jem™* and *The Holograms™*.

*Always on the lookout for new talent, Jem™ and the girls visit a new cabaret. Appearing there is a new group from West Germany, The Stingers™. Jem™, like everyone else, is taken in by the handsome Riot™, the lead singer. Poor Jem™ has already had enough trouble with her dual identity. Outside of The Holograms™, only the President of the United States knows about Synergy™. As Jerrica™, her relation-ship with Rio Pacheco™ (the boy next door), is con-fusing, as naturally since Rio™ loves her, he would love Jem™ as well. Rio™ feels guilty about these feelings. Now the Jem™ side of Jerrica™ is falling in love with another man, a former military man turned singer, Rory Louellen™, or Riot™. This does not help Jem's™ already confused state. Riot™ is accom-panied by two beautiful girls, Minx™, who lives up to her name, and Rapture™, who is into the occult. While not quite as devilish as The Misfits™, The Stingers™ are, after all, in competition with Jem™ and The Holograms™.*

*Jem™, torn between Rio™ and Riot™, her career as a singer, and her newfound fame as an actress, is destined to have many more exciting adventures.*

*Illustration 11.* Danse™, *a ballerina turned choreographer, plans the fancy footwork of* The Holograms™, *while* Video™ *(cousin of* Clash™*), helps* Jem™ *capture her moves on tape!*

*OPPOSITE PAGE: Illustration 12.* Raya Carmen Alonso™ *became the newest member of* The Holograms™ *in 1987 when* Shana™ *left to pursue a fashion career, but returned.*

The *Jem*™ Project designers have already mapped out the dolls for *The Stingers*™, complete with costumes and fabric swatches when the official word filters down...the *Jem*™ Project is finished, we are abandoning future plans.

No official statement is released by Hasbro until Toy Fair 1988. All traces of *Jem*™ are tastefully removed. As I walked down the hall to the press room, I noticed a *Jem*™ doll posed beautifully on someone's desk. It is all that remains of the once Queen of Dolls!

I am shown Hasbro's new fashion doll *Maxie*™. Playing it very safe this year, *Maxie*™ is *Barbie*® size, and is "just a typical teenage girl." *Maxie*™ is a Southern California teenager who just "hangs out" at the mall with her friends, spending daddy's money and is fashion conscious. While of high quality, she is to me, well, sort of like white bread, especially after the glittery world of *Jem*™.

Perhaps as an adult doll collector it is difficult for me to understand all the particulars. We are told as children that life is not a popularity contest, but in many ways it is. Had "the masses" accepted *Jem*™, she would still be around.

The irony is that once the dolls and clothing were half price, children and parents were buying them like crazy. Sales of the videos increased, and even now I overhear people constantly ask store employees where are the *Jem*™ dolls. Having now owned them, the public seems eager for more. Perhaps if Hasbro had given it one more year...

All of this to me is a fascinating story. It is a tale that comes along only every few decades. Whether you like *Jem*™ or not, her story and that of her creation is a fascinating tale of big business, high finances, creativity and the American public! It was a story that needed to be told! □

Credits:

The author would like to thank Bob Gantz for photographic assistance, and Dick Tahsin for coordinating the backdrops and costumes used in the *Jem*™ shots, and for his fantastic art work of the 1988 *Jem*™ line. Thanks also to the *Jem*™ Project designers who supplied the details for this article.

*Illustration 13.* The big Jem™ promotion of 1987 was Glitter 'N Gold Jem™ and the Glitter 'N Gold Fashions™. This poster packed with the doll and some deluxe fashions depicted her world in high quality art.

*Illustration 14.* Even The Misfits™ had their own poster which depicted them at their nasty best!

* Asterisk denotes doll made of character.
* *Jem*™/*Jerrica Benton*™: A beautiful young woman with a secret identity, *Jem*™ is truly outrageous to behold! Leader of her band, *The Holograms*™, she is all glitter and glamour. Her terrific music, wild stage costumes and shocking pink hair have pushed her to the top of the charts. She is the hottest, most sensational new star to hit the pop music world! However, when she removes the flashing LED earrings, made by her father and given to her by *Synergy*™, she transforms back to the person she really is — *Jerrica Benton*™, the beautiful blonde executive and owner of Starlight Music Corporation™. She also manages Starlight House™ — her foster home for young girls. *Jerrica*™ is a contemporary business woman with high self-esteem. She handles the demands others make of her time with cool confidence — yet trying to handle the battle of her dual personality, especially with boyfriend, *Rio*™, is quite hard as well as time-consuming! *The Hologram*™ members, *Synergy*™ and the President of the United States are the only ones who know that *Jem*™ and *Jerrica*™ are the same person, which is truly outrageous!
* *Kimber Benton*™: A terrific talented keyboard player is *Jem's*™ younger sister, *Kimber*™. *Kimber*™ loves to write songs and when she is doing it, look out! She forgets everything else. Her red hair is characteristic of her impulsiveness and hot temperament, but she does a super job organizing meals at Starlight House™ and sees to it that the girls take their turns at learning how to cook. *Kimber*™ is an extreme romantic and loves to have not one, but two boyfriends!
* *Aja Leith*™: Stunning intelligent athletic *Aja*™ is *Jem's*™ bestfriend. She loves cars and motorcycles and plays a sizzling rock guitar for *The Holograms*™. *Aja's*™ blue hair adds to her Oriental appeal as well as her love for martial arts, especially Aiki-do. As the unofficial Starlight House™ chauffeur, she drives the Starlight girls back and forth to school and makes sure that they get plenty of exercise and play sports. *Aja*™ can be incredibly stubborn and it is hard to change her mind once it is made up, but she has a great sense of humor.
* *Shana Elmsferg*™: A lovely glamorous artistically talented young black woman, *Shana*™ is a super terrific *Hologram*™ guitar player. Not only can she play the guitar, but *Shana*™ also enjoys fashion designing and has created some hot styles for *Jem*™ and *The Holograms*™ (and the Starlight™ girls).
* *Raya Carmen Alonso*™: A witty pretty Latin American who plays the role of drummer for *The Holograms*™. *Raya*™ is a shy sensitive girl who values her friendship with *Jem*™ and *The Holograms*™.
* *Rio Pacheco*™: Handsome purple-haired *Rio*™ is the longtime boyfriend of Jerrica Benton™ and acts as road manager for *Jem*™ and *The Holograms*™. He is extremely attracted to *Jem*™ and has a hard time sorting out his true feelings. (I wonder why!) If he only knew that both of the girls he likes are really one in the same!
* *Synergy*™: The holographic computer created by Emmet Benton™, which can create images of anything. It is the friendly aid to *Jem*™ and *The Holograms*™ in times of trouble as well as in transforming *Jerrica*™ into *Jem*™!
* *Giselle Divorjack (Danse)*™: The beautiful choreographer for *Jem*™ and *The Holograms*™ videos and concerts. *Danse*™ is an accomplished ballerina who takes after her mother, *Nadia*™,

***Illustration 15.*** Jem™ *was queen of her world of licensed products that included cosmetics, a speaker, paper dolls, story books (illustrated by Tom Tierney) and video and cassette tapes. A $10 million advertising campaign promoted* Jem™ *simultaneously worldwide!*

who was a famous ballerina in Russia. Besides dancing and choreographing, *Danse*™ owns and manages Haven House™, a shelter house for runaway children.
* *Emmet Benton*™: *Jem*™ and *Kimber's*™ father who as a scientist, succeeded in linking music and three-dimensional holographic images. As the founder and owner of Starlight Music™, Emmet™ created the record company due to his wife, Jacqui's™, resuming her music career. Emmet™ had a sad and sudden death from cancer after his wife's passing.
* *Jacqui Benton*™: *Jem*™ and *Kimber's*™ beautiful blonde mother who, being a foster child herself, formed Starlight House™ for foster girls and took *Aja*™ and *Shana*™ in when they were young girls. A former singing star, Jacqui™ resumed her career later in life and became famous once again, only to have her success cut short due to a plane crash that resulted in her tragic death. Her memory and talent lives on through her children.

* *Vivien Montgomery*™ (*Video*™): *Jem's*™ personal friend as well as video photographer for *Jem*™ and *The Holograms*™.
* *Anthony Julian*™: The famous black video director who produces and directs *Jem*™ and *The Holograms*™ award-winning videos. *Anthony*™ is also *Shana's*™ good-looking boyfriend!
* *Lindsay Pierce*™: A hip curly-blonde video hostess (ala "MTV") who helps *Jem*™ and *The Holograms*™ with publicity for the group.
* *Jeff Wright*™: *Kimber's*™ blonde boyfriend who is a Hollywood stuntman. The two met on the set of *Jem's*™ film, *Starbright*.
* *Shawn Harrison*™: The British teen idol who is known for his singing, songwriting and acting. He is *Kimber's*™ brunette boyfriend as well as songwriting collaborator. *Shawn*™ has also co-starred with *Jem*™ in the film *Starbright*.
* *Phyllis Gabor*™ (*Pizazz*™): The green-haired temptress/leader of *The Misfits*™, the "bad girl group" who rivals *Jem*™ and the *Holograms*™. *Pizazz*™ poses as lead singer and guitarist for the

**Illustration 16.** *Hollywood Jem™, the lead doll conceived but never made for 1988, in the basic costume the doll was to be sold in. (The original workroom sketches have been reworked by artist Dick Tahsin.)*

group and is extremely jealous of *Jem™*. She will do **anything** to soil her reputation and is constantly trying to seduce *Jem's™* boyfriend, *Rio™*. *Pizazz™* is a cruel, spoiled, rich, vicious, vain, unsympathetic creature who takes out her anger, for her mother having left her and her wealthy father at an early age, on everyone around her.

* *Mary Phillips™ (Stormer™)*: The girl with a "heart" who is guitarist/composer for *The Misfits™*. *Stormer™* is the nicer of the four girls who comprise *The Misfits™* and has even formed a friendship with *Kimber Benton™*!

* *Roxanne Pellegrini™ (Roxy™)*: The sassy platinum blonde of *The Misfits™*, who is a native of South Philadelphia. *Roxy™* is a wise gum-crackin' gal who dropped out of school at an early age and has never learned how to read. She is the epitome of "the bad girl from the wrong side of the tracks!" *Roxy™* is in constant search of wealth, fame and material possessions, evidently because she never grew up with such things.

* *Sheila Thompson™ (Jetta™)*: The Misfits'™ British import who plays a wicked saxophone! *Jetta™* comes from the poor part of England, yet she poses as having nobility and being a British Aristocrat. A raven-haired beauty, *Jetta™* is the comedienne of *The Misfits™* and can always be heard saying "luv" or "ducky"!

* *Constance Montgomery™ (Clash™)*: The evil cousin of *Video™* who wishes desperately to become the fifth member of *The Misfits™*. *Clash™* uses a variety of disguises to do her dirty deeds against *Jem™* and *The Holograms™*. In fact, she has even gone so far as to impersonate *Jem™* herself!

* *Eric Raymond™*: Former co-chief executive of Starlight Music™ who now manages Misfit Music™. *Eric™* is downright evil when it comes to money and power, as well as carrying out his vendetta against *Jerrica Benton™* for overtaking Starlight Music™ from him.

* *Tek-Rat™*: An unscrupulous menace who is constantly employed by *Eric Raymond™* to wreck havoc for *Jem™* and *The Holograms™*.

* *Harvey Gabor™*: *Pizazz's™* millionaire father who will give her anything to keep her out of his hair. Little does he know that what she really needs is his love and attention, something she never got as a child.

* *Craig Philips™*: A blue-haired hunk, who is *Stormer's™* estranged brother and *Aja's™* love interest. *Craig™* is a great drummer and competed along with *Raya™* for the drummer title for *Jem™* and *The Holograms™*.

* *Countess Danielle DuBoisin™*: A high society designer who loves to support *Jem™* and *The Holograms™*. She has thrown parties on her

**Illustration 17.** *The lead dolls for 1988 would have been* The Stingers™. *Dressed in their stage costumes they are* Minx™ *(modeled after model Jerry Hall, in my opinion),* Riot™, *the charismatic lead singer and* Rapture™. *This group was replacing* The Misfits™. *Riot™ was also a new love interest for* Jem™*! (The original workroom sketches have been reworked by artist Dick Tahsin.)*

*Illustration 18. Another surprising 1988 doll was another friend for Jem™, Regine Cesaré™, a fashion designer from Martinique, shown in the outfit she would have been sold in. She would have been made from the Raya™ mold, but with the blue hair of Aja™! (The original workroom sketches have been reworked by artist Dick Tahsin.)*

magnificent yacht in honor of *Jem*™ and the girls and has even designed spectacular fashions especially for them!

* *Harriett Horne*™: The queen barracuda of rock gossip who hosts a talk show where she "barbecues the stars"!

### 1988 New Characters and Would-be Dolls

* Denotes that a doll was **planned** on being made of the character.

* *Regine Cezaré*™: A successful young Martinique/Parisian fashion designer who was imported to the United States by *Countess Du-Boisin*™. *Regine*™ uses her creative talent and becomes the official costume designer for *Jem*™ and *The Holograms*™, although she was lured away briefly by *The Stingers*™.

* *Astral*™: A beautiful raven-haired magician with magical, mystical powers!

* *Rory Louellen*™ *(Riot*™*):* The founder and lead singer of the new West German imported rock group, *The Stingers*™, who have taken the United States by storm! *Riot*™ is an egotistical long-haired muscular blonde God, whom women find irresistible. He causes a "riot" wherever he goes and whenever his group performs. *Riot's*™ macho-military father was against his becoming a musician and urged him to join the army, which he did. Stationed in Germany, *Riot*™ soon found his love for music resurfacing and quit the army to form his own group. *Pizazz*™ is infatuated with *Riot*™, yet he wants only the girl he is in love with — *Jem*™! He vows one day to make her his!

* *Minx*™: The Lolita/sexpot of *The Stingers*™ who plays synthesizer for the group. A native of West Germany, *Minx*™ claims she can get any man and has her sights on *Rio*™! Her and her co-hort, *Rapture's*™, evil antics make *The Misfits*™ look like Pollyanna!

* *Rapture*™: The guitarist of *The Stingers*™, *Rapture*™ is deep into the occult and claims she possesses mystical powers.

The following are registered trademarks of Hasbro, Inc.: Starlight House™, Jem™, The Holograms™, The Misfits™, Shana™, Raya Carmen Alonso™, Starlight Music™, Kimber Benton™, Kimber™, Hollywood Jem™, Hollywood Jem™ Fashions™, Glitter 'N Gold™, Regine Cezaré™, Raya™, Regine™, The Stingers™, Riot™, Synergy™ Jerrica™, Rio™, Rory Louellen™, Minx™, Rapture™, Maxie™, Danse™, Video™, Clash™, Glitter 'N Gold Jem™, Glitter 'N Gold Fashions™, Aja™, Rob™, Jerrica Benton™, Aja Leith™, Shana Elmsferg™, Rio Pacheco™, Giselle Divorjack™, Nadia™, Haven House™, Emmet Benton™, Jacqui Benton™, Vivien Montgomery™, Anthony Julian™, Lindsay Pierce™, Jeff Wright™, Shawn Harrison™, Phyllis Gabor™, Pizazz™, Mary Philips™, Stormer™, Roxanne Pellegrini™, Roxy™, Sheila Thompson™, Jetta™, Constance Montgomery™, Clash™, Eric Raymond™, Misfit Music™, Tek-Rat™, Harvey Gabor™, Craig Philips™, Countess Danielle DuBoisin™, Harriett Horne™, Astral™.

*Barbie*® and *Ken*® are registered trademarks of Mattel, Inc.

*Illustration 19. For 1988 Hasbro went back to basics. Its entry into the fashion doll market is Maxie™ and her boyfriend, Rob™. They are typical Southern California teens and Barbie® and Ken® size. While well done, they lack the sizzling power of Jem™ and her world.*

**Illustration 1.** In 1982, amid much fanfare LJN Toys, Ltd., introduced the Barbie -size doll Brooke Shields®...She's a Doll which was a wonderful likeness of the famous teenage fashion model. The company handed out buttons at Toy Fair which said "Go for Brooke" to promote the product.

# Brooke Shields — She's A Doll!

Standing almost 6 feet, with an astonishing face, bearing its famous hawk-wing eyebrows, deep blue eyes, full lips and topped off by a signature brunette mane, her beauty is a rare breed and not seen more than once or twice in a decade. As photographer Francesco Scavullo says, "She was born beautiful, she stays beautiful, and she gets more beautiful every month." She is Brooke Shields.

Born May 31, 1965, Brooke has literally grown up before our eyes from adorable Ivory Soap baby to sophisticated *Vogue* cover girl. Over the past 23 years, Brooke has transformed into quite a star!

The one person solely responsible for both the private and the public phenomenon of Brooke Shields is mother-manager Teri Shields, who gave birth to Brooke at 31, three months before divorcing socialite Frank Shields. Teri began molding, marketing and managing Brooke's career from the time her daughter was born. She began trotting Brooke around to photographers' studios (namely Francesco Scavullo's!) before the child could talk in sentences, posed her for Ivory Soap before age one, had her cast in her first movie, *Alice Sweet Alice*, when she was nine and pushed her forward at 11 for the controversial role of the child prostitute in Louis Malle's film *Pretty Baby*. One magazine wrote that "Teri plans Brooke's career the way Eisenhower planned D-day." Still, despite the fact that she engineered her daughter's rise to fame without any previous business

*ABOVE RIGHT: Illustration 2. In 1983, Brooke was graduating from high school, and LJN Toys, Ltd., capitalized on this with* Prom Party Brooke Shields,® *a stunningly gowned version of the doll. The beautiful long hair was the best feature.*

*Illustration 3. The basic doll, on the left, came with an autographed picture of Brooke Shields. The doll on the right is* Suntan Brooke Shields,® *another version of the doll that is very hard to find today.*

**LEFT: Illustration 4.** Prom Party Brooke Shields® *mint-in-the-box. In the Philadelphia area, only Kay-Bee stores stocked this doll, and then just for a short time.*

**RIGHT: Illustration 5.** *The fashions for the doll were pretty basic and not Mattel quality, but the point was to undersell Mattel with a personality that was real instead of a fantasy character like Barbie®! The problem is that fantasy characters do not grow up quite as fast!*

experience, Teri is frequently seen as the ultimate stage mother, manipulative and overly protective. "I think Mom's very much misunderstood," Brooke told *Cosmopolitan* magazine. "It baffles me that she's not given the credit she deserves. People say she's protective, but she's really just looking out for me." Brooke and Teri's relationship of model puppet and master puppeteer was clearly seen on the 1984 ABC television series "Paper Dolls." The drama series focused on the glittering high-powered world of fashion and told the story of teen superstar model Taryn Blake who yearns for a normal teenage life, yet is always reaching for greater success, driven by her ambitious mother-manager, Julia Blake. The similarity between the "fictitious" television story and the real-life one was amazing! The only difference being that Brooke NEVER yearned for a normal teenage life: she always had it along with her superstar status. In fact, Brooke says she has never been robbed of her childhood. "There's never been a time when I've said I just want to be a kid, because all along I have been just a kid."

**Illustration 6.** *A carry case was made for the doll and clothing. These items are just now disappearing from stores after being marked down to cost. The prudent collector waits for these opportunities to buy future collectibles at half price!*

In the early 1980s, Brooke gained stardom as a model/actress at a very young age, appearing on such magazine covers as *Cosmopolitan*, *Vogue* and *Harper's Bazaar* as well as starring in films like *Blue Lagoon* and *Endless Love*. Her one million dollar contract, in 1981, with Calvin Klein to model his jeans at age 16 was a landmark, as were the "naughty" television ads. In the commercials a coltish tempting Brooke asks, "Wanna know what comes be-

**Illustration 7.** *The real Brooke Shields certainly proves...she's a doll!* Photograph by Movie Star News.

tween me and my Calvins? Nothing!" The ads caused quite a sensation!

Brooke's known personality as a bright, genuinely nice, no-nonsense girl who was a high school cheerleader and honor student, as well as fashion model and actress, took America by storm. The fascination with Brooke and her "*Barbie*®-like" life intrigued many, especially young girls. For now there was finally a "REAL" *Barbie*® to look up to and not just a doll!

In 1982, LJN Toys, Ltd., issued the *Brooke Shields*® doll for which Brooke received a reported one million dollars for the rights to produce such an item. LJN Toys, Ltd., also promised another one million dollars in advertisements. Quite a hefty sum for a 17-year-old! The 11½in (29cm) vinyl doll was a high quality product and really captured the "Brooke look" complete with Wella Balsam hair, full lips and thick brows! The doll came dressed in a ribbed turtleneck and tights with boots and included an autographed picture of Brooke signed "With love, Brooke Shields." Unlike her blonde rival, *Barbie*,® the *Brooke*® doll had underpants that were painted-on for she was much too proper to be totally bare! Brooke was seen with the doll on "The Johnny Carson Show" and in *Time* magazine in February of 1982. Her comment on the doll was "Wind it up and it goes to school!"

Capitalizing on her fashion career, the doll's tag line read, "The world's most glamorous teenager" and had a *Glamour Center* play setting as well as an entire line of clothing called *Brooke's High Fashion Ensemble*. The ensemble consisted of two lines, *Funtime Fashions* and *Designer Boutique*, which ran the gamut from cheerleader and horse rider to roller skater and cowgirl with many more styles in between.

In 1982, LJN Toys, Ltd., made a second version of the Brooke doll in *Suntan Brooke Shields*® which came in a darker skin tone and showcased a yellow bikini along with a new smiling face, which differed from the original doll's closed-mouth look.

In 1983, Brooke was 18 and a senior at Swight-Englewood High School in New Jersey. She now had the glorious

moment of graduation and the senior prom to look forward to and indeed she did! LJN Toys, Ltd., also looked forward to the two events, especially the latter, and in 1983 issued *Prom Party Brooke Shields*® to tie into with Brooke's real-life event. The doll came dressed in a magenta prom gown and shoulder wrap and sported the smiling face previously shown on the suntan version of the doll. The doll was exceptionally well made and is very hard to locate today. It seems everyone loved Brooke as a Prom Queen and snatched this version of the doll up quickly! Brooke attended her prom with her escort, model/actor Ted McGinley of "Love Boat" and "Dynasty" fame. The two looked radiant together and the news media picked this up, calling them the real-life *Barbie*® and *Ken*®! It appeared to be the gossip scoop of the decade; Brooke FINALLY had a romance! The two, however, were just

good friends and to this day, Brooke has been without a hot show-biz romance to reveal, though that could change soon.

In the fall of 1983, Brooke pranced off to Princeton to earn a college degree in English Literature, which she proudly received in May of 1987. She went from the world's most glamourous teenager to the world's most famous college student!

Today Brooke, now 24, is almost as much a legend as her recent screen character "Brenda Starr" and with her college degree and her success as the glamourous redheaded comic strip heroine, there will be no stopping this multifaceted young woman, for she is indeed a doll! □

*Barbie*® and *Ken*® are registered trademarks of Mattel, Inc.
*Brooke Shields,*® *Suntan Brooke Shields*® and *Prom Party Brooke Shields*® are registered trademarks of LJN Toys, Ltd.

# The Alexander Doll Company — An American Tradition Continues

Photographs by **Paul Sackett**

*"CHANGE...Repeating the same thing in different ways"*
*Charles Dickens*

***Illustration 1.*** *Madame Alexander introduces Jeff Chodorow and Ira Smith, new owners of the Alexander Doll Company.*

Every year, like the little boy who cries wolf, rumors abound about the almost mythical Alexander Doll Company. With Madame Alexander now 93 years old and still very active, fans of this 65-year-old firm have wondered for years, often with dread, what would happen to the beloved dolls they have cherished for generations.

Saturday, February 7th, was a historic day for all those interested in dolls. The famed Alexander Doll Company changed ownership, with controlling shares purchased by two men who themselves sparked intense curiosity. Collectors, dealers and just fans of the Alexander doll firm were eager to know just what this change in ownership would mean for the future!

Gary R. Ruddell, publisher of **Doll Reader**® and Chairman of the Board of IDA (the International Doll Academy which produces the prestigious Dolls Of The Year® awards), recently had an opportunity to meet with the new primary owners of the company and hear of their plans for the future. During this interview, the new owners and Mr. Ruddell talked at length about the past, present and future of the Alexander Doll Company.

The story of Madame Alexander is indeed a fascinating one. Born over a doll hospital opened in 1885 by her father, a Russian immigrant, young Beatrice Alexander acquired early an eye for beauty. She saw with regret the tears in the eyes of little girls whose porcelain dolls had been broken. When

World War I made the lovely German dolls impossible to obtain, Beatrice and her three sisters began to "manufacture" cloth dolls, the first of which was a *Red Cross Nurse*. During 1923, Madame made a doll of her daughter, Mildred, and with the encouragement of her husband, Phillip Behrman, opened the Alexander Doll Company.

By 1960, the company employed over 600 persons. With "Madame" (a nickname acquired because of her distinctive and ladylike way of doing business) at the helm, the business blossomed.

The new primary owners, both businessmen and attorneys, are from the New York area. Jeff Chodorow is Chairman of the Board and Ira Smith is Vice Chairman of the Board. President of the company is William Birnbaum, Madame Alexander's grandson.

The interesting news to fans of Madame Alexander is that she is to remain with the company in the capacity of consultant. Not having to worry about the running of the business any longer has actually given Madame much more time to do what she does best...design! In fact, the new owners say that Madame corresponds with them daily from her West Palm Beach home and has been to New York several times since February. Collectors can breathe a sigh of relief, for Madame plans to remain active in the company indefinitely, offering her years of experience and wisdom as well as her artistic eye.

*tration 2.* Ruth Albistor, a designer for the Alexander Doll *ipany for 35 years, and her co-designer, Mariana Pellegrino.*

**Illustration 3.** *William Birnbaum, President of the Alexander Doll Company and grandson of Madame Alexander, with Jay Schwartz, Sales Manager of the Alexander Doll Company.*

# Hair Treatment

An interesting fact about the company is that most of the employees have a 20, 30, even 40 year history with the firm, which speaks highly of the way business is conducted. The dolls are made in the United States and plans are to keep it that way!

Jeff Chodorow is proud to say that although Madame Alexander was offered more money by others, she was so convinced that he and Mr. Smith cared about the product and would continue the traditions of the company, that she sold it to them!

One change that will occur is with the allocation (distribution) of dolls to dealers. The supply of Alexander dolls has never met the demand. The new owners feel that not much expansion is feasible. Supervisors of production keep quality high, and to add more sewers, and make more dolls, would jeopardize the standards for which the Alexander Doll Company has been known.

Jeff Chodorow, along with the Board, explains that the new system will mean that dealers will be allotted the number of dolls which the new owners feel they can supply. A problem in the past has been that orders were taken above the level of dolls produced. The new allocation system is a complicated step, but one the new owners feel will benefit everyone.

The years 1987 and 1988 were and are exciting ones at the Alexander Doll Company. The reintro-

*Illustration 4. A group of dolls in mid coiffure.*

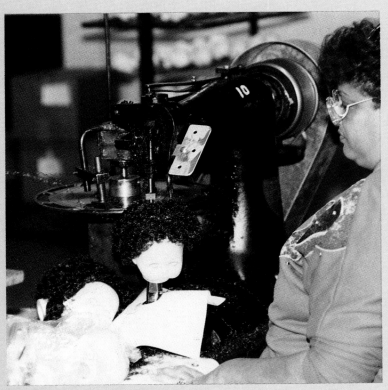

*Illustration 5. A worker in the Alexander factory stitches on doll wigs.*

duction of the *Portrettes*, first made in 1968, and discontinued in 1973, made collectors take notice of a real return to the old standards of quality. The famous 8in (20cm) *Alexander-kins* also got a wonderful new standard mold that is a twin to the way they looked in 1954; the return of the *Maggie* smiling face on these little dolls, first developed in 1960, is a welcome addition.

Do the new owners see any real changes? All the men agreed that baby dolls are taking the spotlight once again as the mothers of today want their daughters to have more "traditional" dolls than have been available. The men quoted production records that show during the *Cabbage Patch Kids*™ phenomenon, and the "talking" doll craze, Alexander baby doll sales were still far above their ability to produce enough to satisfy the demand.

Ira Smith feels, along with the entire Board, that the time has come to possibly expand the baby doll category to compete more thoroughly with the European market. With the dollar down, imports are increasingly more expensive, and the new owners, like Madame always did, see an opportunity to capture an expanding market.

It was Madame's ability to predict that the Dionne Quintuplets would be the "Darlings of the Depression" that really put the company on top.

*Illustration 6.* *A close-up view of the hair being set on an Alexander doll's head.*

*Illustration 7.* *A worker in the Alexander factory making dolls' hats.*

The new owners, continuing that wonderful keen eye of entrepreneurship, see the new generation of children as only slightly different than their predecessors.

All the owners feel that the image of "untouchable" dolls was more important to the 1950s child than to those of today. One of the changes they envision is American-made play value to some of the Alexander dolls. A child should be able to enjoy a doll and make that doll a part of her life.

Interesting information was exchanged during the discussion about manufacturing techniques. Collectors have wondered why some dolls of the past seem so difficult to find today. Jeff Chodorow

# Dressing

*Illustration 8.* *A group of dolls from the* First Ladies *series showing their beautiful gowns.*

explained that sometimes fabric ordered runs out and cannot be obtained again. Rather than change the fabric, often the doll has been silently discontinued. Thus, while still shown in the catalog, it actually was not made or shipped in great quantities! Collectors welcome this "tidbit" as the older dolls are continually in demand on the collectors' market.

Gone, however, is the speculative buying which drove up prices on the "secondary" market on currently made dolls. Jay Schwartz, Sales Manager of the company, and the others are glad those days are over. For almost 15 years Alexander dolls were conspicuously absent from stores, having been snapped up the day they arrived by eager collectors and dealers who often waited in line for hours to purchase the three-doll limit many stores had! This meant that two generations of little girls grew up without seeing many Alexander dolls in the stores! Thankfully, children again can go with their parents or grandparents to fine stores, and pick out their Christmas or birthday dolls. The new owners feel that dolls are an entire year business. Collectors buy throughout the year as well as holidays, and a baby doll often is bought on eye appeal with no special reason in mind.

At the conclusion of the interview, Gary Ruddell could not help but ask what specific plans for the coming years the men have. While not revealing specifics, all commented that because perhaps as many as 100 dolls a year are designed, but only 30 to 40 new dolls are produced there is quite a ponderous

*Illustration 9.* *A seamstress holding up a tiny tutu in preparation to adding beadwork.*

## Shoes

*Illustration 10. Seaming and stitching doll shoes at the Alexander Doll factory.*

file of Madame Alexander's beautiful creations to draw from in the future. Obviously, the company is one that is full of life, creativity and satisfaction from a job well done, pleasing both the collector and the child.

The final question: With all the famous anniversaries coming up such as *Gone With the Wind, The Wizard of Oz* (both films turn 50 next year), AND renewed interest in celebrities of the past such as the Dionnes, do any of these events figure in future plans? The men, like Madame always did, smile and say they do not know for sure.

One thing we do know for sure is that the Alexander Doll Company is going to continue the rich creative traditions that made it the leader in American-made dolls for 65 years! It is comforting for all who have loved and cherished both Madame Alexander and her exquisite dolls that her motto, "A Thing of Beauty Is a Joy Forever" is going to continue to delight present and future generations of children and collectors. Many today owe their early exposure to the fine arts to this grand lady. In our fast changing world, Madame Alexander represents the ideal of quality American-made products by people who care, delivered proudly to those who love them! □

*Cabbage Patch Kids*™ is a trademark of Original Appalachian Artworks, Inc., Cleveland, Georgia, U.S.A. All Rights Reserved.

**Illustration 11.** *A close-up of a sole being glued onto a doll shoe.*

**Illustration 12.** *Tito Castro, General Manager of the Alexander Doll Company, holds a box of snaps used on the Alexander doll shoes.*

# Lady Luminous

As a Contributing Editor to **Doll Reader**, one of my jobs is to search the world for new exciting collectibles of which readers need to be aware.

Recently, a very lifelike and extremely well-made doll has been causing a sensation in Japan, and is now beginning to be noticed here by collectors of fine dolls.

The Takara Toy Company, certainly no stranger to quality, is responsible for manufacturing a high fashion mannequin-type doll that is so breathtakingly real it is uncanny.

In November 1988, Takara introduced *Petite Mannequin*. The doll, made of top quality vinyl with painted features and luxurious hair, stands 17in (43cm) high and is jointed at the neck and arms. The legs are posed in the typical model's stance of one foot forward, giving a "runway" type of modeling look to the doll. The company rapidly changed the doll to *Deux-L*, which in French means two "L's," and the new formal name on the box is *Lady Luminous*.

Takara claims the doll is completely realistic, with real fashion model proportions of the ideal body size: 68in (172cm) tall, 21in (53cm) waist and 34in (86cm) hips.

The real outstanding feature of these dolls is the wardrobe. Not since the "glory days" of Mattel and Madame Alexander has so much craftsmanship gone into clothing. The entire ensemble has been coordinated from head to toe, with a hair style and color to match the ensemble, makeup done in the correct tones, and careful attention to seam and hem finishes on lavish fabrics. Last but not least, the proper hose and jewelry are selected so that each *Lady Luminous* doll represents a miniature runway model down to the last minute detail.

Adding to the high quality is the exquisitely plain heavy cardboard box in which the dolls come. The name "*Lady Luminous*" is embossed in gold, and the name Takara is not even on the box! The doll's feet and shoes have holes in them into which two rods on a round chrome base fit, much the way the first *Barbie* stands worked. If I had to rate this product on a quality scale of one to ten, ten would NOT suffice.

In an article in *Barbie Bazaar* magazine, Sumiko Watanabe reported that the dolls are not only available in toy and doll shops, but in plastic model shops, for Takara estimates that 70 percent of its sales are to adult MEN! Yes, it seems as if a number of young men in Japan are interested in the world of fashion, but for many reasons were not encouraged, and thus find *Deux-L*, an outlet for their creativity. Many of these men, Sumiko reports, are about 30 years old and are office workers. They are repainting the facial features

***Illustration 1.*** *The face of the 1990s,* Lady Luminous, *the new Takara fashion doll for Japan, has the makeup of the 1990s, with a very 1960s Vidal Sasson hair style and heavy globe earrings.*

and designing wardrobes for the dolls.

Last year, Takara introduced boxed clothing for the dolls that included sexy lingerie and most of the ensembles that came on the dolls. Again, the name Takara did not appear on the boxes!

*Lady Luminous* comes in a white version, a suntan version and a brown skin tone model.

While researching this article, after first learning of the dolls from Sumiko, I found that information was very difficult to obtain.

A call to the Takara Company in New York was fruitless. The person I spoke with had never heard of the doll. Since the name Takara is not on the box, I wondered if indeed Takara was the manufacturer, but an airline steward friend of mine brought me a doll that had a warranty card inside with the Takara name on it.

The doll is quite expensive, both in Japanese and American money. Some dealers here are importing the dolls from various sources and charging anywhere from $195 to $495! The dolls have suddenly, in the last few months, gained great appeal. Much of this appeal is with *Barbie* collectors, who would naturally gravitate to a fashion mannequin, and another part of the desirability of the dolls is their difficulty to locate. Collectors always seem to want what is scarce, and since these dolls are such a hot item in Japan, they are not always available in stores when airline personnel are in town! This "thrill of the hunt" is in every collector's blood!

The history of the fashion doll goes back centuries, but over the past 31 years, *Barbie* has been the main source of study to document the revolutionary changes in fashion.

Now with a new doll that is dressed up-to-the-minute and selling well, it seems that fashion will be documented three-dimensionally by *Lady Luminous* as well!

The phenomenon of men entering the fashion doll field makes some a bit nervous, but at a recent doll show, I met a gentleman whose views summed it up quite well. This man, a veteran of Vietnam, now working at a "boring but well

*Illustration 2.* Lady Luminous' hair styles, makeup and fashions all coordinate beautifully with each other. The author did not style the hair...it came already beauty shop fresh!

*Illustration 3.* A brown-skinned doll sports a pulled-back cascade of curls, and a red velvet floor-length gown with red fur trim. The quality is astonishing.

*Illustration 4.* Full-length view of the brown-skinned Deux-L showing her model's pose and chrome stand. The proportions of the doll equal that of a real live fashion model.

*Illustration 5.* Full-length view of the doll seen in Illustration 1. The shoes are spectator pumps and the dress is very retro 1960s.

*Illustration 6. A haughty top fashion model look for* **Lady Luminous** *who has long straight hair and wears a checked blazer with a polka dot pocket square, and a chic mini with dark hose.* **Marl Davidson Collection.**

*Illustration 7. This is my favorite doll! The hair style in this doll is hand done with spiked bangs, twisted sides and a long straight back. Her padded-shoulder blazer offsets her silk blouse with "LL" embroidered on it.*

paying" corporate job, and the father of three children, had always wanted to be a fashion designer, but 30 years ago his family refused his repeated requests for assistance to pursue that career. This man obviously had his creativity stifled and now is making up for lost time, sketching and designing for *Lady Luminous* dolls. If some of you women find this strange, ask yourself what YOUR options were 30 or 40 years ago! How many little girls who would have made brilliant car mechanics or even doctors were discouraged by a society which, thankfully, recognizes today that we all are individuals with the potential to be virtually anyone and anything we put our minds to!

The last point I would like to make about these lovely dolls is a bit sad. Everyone who has seen these dolls says the same thing. Why are dolls like this unavailable in the United States? The sad truth is that the Japanese demand a higher quality product than we Americans do. If you doubt this, let me remind you of another Takara doll, *Lisa*, which was sold here for several years in the early 1980s. Do you remember? Of course not! The doll was like every other cheaply coiffed and dressed doll found in chain toy stores, but in Japan, the Takara company made *Lisa* (only she was called *Licca*) with a quality not seen here in decades. Elaborately coiffed and dressed, she came in gift sets, and had a color catalog that would rival the finest fashion magazines! When I asked at Toy Fair why the quality difference, the shy polite Japanese man bowed his head and said, "Forgive me, but you Americans simply do not require the quality." I have never forgotten that encounter, and it left me feeling sad that we as a nation had such a reputation.

Obviously from the way *Lady Luminous* is selling here on the secondary market, Americans ARE willing to pay for and do desire quality, and have it they do, in the most gorgeous of fashion dolls to come along in decades.

Fashion dolls are interesting not only because they are well made, or marketed, but in the future serve so well to tell the story of 20th century dress. Like the old French fashions of long ago, a new "French fashion" by the name of *Deux-L* is right now telling what is hot in the ever-changing world of fashion. ☐

Authors note: One of the objectives of the DOTY* (Dolls of the Year*) program, sponsored by Hobby House Press, Inc., is to expand the meaning of the word "doll." To many, the word represents merely a baby doll to train a little girl to be a good mommy. While that certainly can and should be part of the definition of a doll, as a member of the Board of Directors of DOTY, I am proud to be one of many who want the word "doll" elevated to the status that it should have. With all the fine artists', manufacturers', antique and collectors' dolls, the definition of the word doll definitely needs expanding. Doll collecting is now a part of fine art, and anyone, regardless of age, race or gender can join the fun! Help make doll collecting a hobby for EVERYONE!

**Illustration 8.** *Full-length view showing the entire "Dynasty" type of outfit.*

**Illustration 9.** *Step into the 1990s with this chic Duex-L with blonde ponytail, black suit and Roman coin jewelry.*

*Barbie* is a registered trademark for Mattel, Inc.

# STARR and Her High School Friends

**Illustration 2.** *The Springfield High School gang, class of 1981. From left to right they are:* Kelley™, *the smart one;* Starr™, *the girl with it all; the boyfriend,* Shaun™; *and* Tracy™, *the zany friend.*

High school is a time in one's life when many changes occur. It should be a time when one is attractive, healthy and full of curiosity about the world. It is a time to have fun. Youth has, through high school, an opportunity to learn, but also to have adventures and experiment to find the person you would like to become. Many children look forward to high school years with joy and anticipation of the dates, dances, clothing and social activites these years bring. Some, however, perhaps those with less social skills, or less attractive looks, dread these years and often do not take full advantage of the opportunities presented. "Learning" how to be a teenager is an awesome lesson that needs much preparation. Dolls are one way through which these lessons can be learned.

In the late 1970s, the Disco dance craze, as well as the popularity of the Baby Boomers (now in their late 20s), focused the attention of the doll world on fashion dolls that could hardly be teenagers. Kenner's *Darci* (for more information on *Darci,* see *"Darci Fever"* by A. Glenn Mandeville in the November 1987 **Doll Reader** pages 150 to 158 and friends were sort of like *Charlie's Angels,* that is women, not teens. Mattel's *Barbie* and *Ken*, once the epitome of "teendom," had, in my opinion, aged considerably. *Superstar Barbie* and *Ken* certainly did not inhabit the halls of high school. They were stars of the nightclubs, and therefore had to be at least 21. From the splendor of the life they

*Illustration 1. Starr™ and her boyfriend, Shaun™, exemplify the best of high school life in 1980! This illustration is shot against a Starr™ paper doll book.*

*Illustration 3.* *Cheerleading and sports are important at Springfield High. Here* Kelley™ *and* Tracy™ *model* Cheerleader Captain *while* Starr™ *and* Shaun™ *wear matching track suits.*

*Illustration 4.* *There is always time for a 1950s dance at Springfield High! Here* Starr™ *and* Kelley™ *model* School Days! *in front of a record by Fabian.*

led, 25 or 30 would be more an appropriate age!

Children simply did not have a "role model," as it were, anymore to introduce them, not to the distant future but the immediate future. *Barbie* was no longer "Queen of the Prom." She was queen of an ADULT world.

Interestingly, focus was turning backward to teenagers as the decade of the 1980s dawned. The Baby Boomers, now in their late 20s (as mentioned previously), were (and still are) getting all the attention, but the new group was coming up, still technically Baby Boomers. These were raised in a freer, more liberal atmosphere than the early boom children. These children were often referred to as "latchkey" children, or youngsters who came home to an empty house, as mother now worked out of necessity instead of baking cookies all day long. Divorce was commonplace; life styles such as living together before marriage were something children were exposed to on a daily basis.

Many saw profit, in my opinion, in exploiting the troubles that this generation, namely those in their teens in the early 1980s, seemed to have. Drugs, sexual promiscuity, teen pregnancy, "finding onself," suicide, violence and depression were often the theme of movies about these "lost souls." Particularly obnoxious were the movies dubbed "teen slaughter" movies which usually focused on some poor teenage girl and her unfortunate friends who, while being in adult situations, found themselves victims of some psychopathic murderer!

The child coming up during all this "negative attention" needed desperately to find some role models of active moral fun-loving teens. It seemed that these were very hard to find!

Mattel, always possessing the uncanny ability to predict future trends, saw this need emerge in children. Just like *Barbie* would show the frightened prepubescent girl of the late 1950s, all the secrets of teendom, so would the new "star" at Mattel do the same for the preteen of the early 1980s!

With much fanfare, Mattel announced in 1980 a series of new dolls, simply called *Starr ..and Her High School Friends.*

*ABOVE: Illustration 5.* The movie Roller Boogie, *in 1979, starring Jim Bray, on the left, and Linda Blair, showed teens much like* Starr™ *and* Shaun™. *The dolls came with roller skates just like those shown!* Photograph courtesy of Movie Star News, a United Artist Releae, 1979.

*RIGHT: Illustration 6. To help stores promote* Starr™, *Mattel distributed a beautiful store display which contained* Starr™ *in a lucite star. The background was a very imaginative notebook paper design. These store displays are highly collectible and add to the fun of doll collecting.*

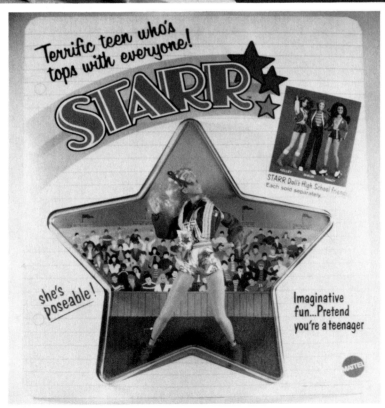

The name, *Starr*, said it all. *Starr* possessed many of the same characteristics that *Barbie* had possessed in 1959, but was not quite the glowing superhuman person that *Barbie* was. *Starr* was basically just an upper middle class teenage girl whose parents supported her. Packed with the doll was a description of *Starr*. "Like in most high schools, there is one girl who's everyone's favorite. She's pretty. She's got a wonderful personality. She's smart. And she's good at sports. At Springfield High, that girl is *Starr*. She's 'the girl with everything.' Everyone loves her."

Before the reader gags on the sheer perfection of this person, remember that *Barbie*, in 1959, was described much the same way, only on top of all that, she was a globe-trotting highly successful top fashion model. At least *Starr* was merely a "normal" girl, whose abilities would be defined by educators as "gifted."

Americans have always loved their fantasies about "idealized" life. Actress Donna Reed, before her recent death, recalled feeling guilty that she made an entire nation of mothers feel bad about themselves because they could not live up to her television mother image. Miss Reed recalled that hours of grooming, makeup and set decorating created the "illusion" that became the standard for an entire generation of children and adults raised on "The Donna Reed Show." Even today, when only 25 percent of the houses we ride by contain a married couple with children, we fantasize about the "happy" family that must live inside all these homes!

It has always been my opinion that these fantasies are healthy when viewed as a goal and role model, while at the same time realizing that perfection is impossible, but a nice thing for which to strive. We get into trouble when we berate ourselves for not COMPLETELY living up to these perfect models.

*Starr* was not alone in her image. Her male counterpart, *Shaun*, was described as such in the Springfield High School Yearbook, packed with all the dolls and lavishly illustrated: "He's the guy every girl wants to date. *Shaun* is not only handsome, he's smart, fun, and a great athlete, too. He seems to do everything well and easily." Not too hard to live up to, right! Yet the pre-adolescent, afraid of watching teenagers self-destruct in movies or burn out on drugs on television, needed some real heroes to look up to. In fact HERO seems to be a word lost to this generation. When thinking of the 1950s or 1960s one can come up with many images of famous people with whom to compare *Barbie*. In fact the author did just that in *Doll Fashion Anthology and Price Guide* (published by Hobby House Press, Inc.). All throughout *Barbie's* long life it has been easy to tie her in

***Illustration 7.*** *As was Mattel policy at the time, department stores carried a deluxe version of* Starr™ *which came with a record. This would be worth about $35.00 today.*

***Illustration 8.*** *Basic* Starr™ *and* Shaun™ *dolls.* Starr™ *came packed with teenage accoutrements such as schoolbooks and a tambourine.* Shaun™ *came with a guitar.*

**Illustration 9.** *Basic* Tracy™ *and* Kelley™ *dolls. The story on the packaging was as interesting as the dolls themselves. Packed with each doll was an incredibly photographed Springfield High School Yearbook (copyright 1979 by Mattel), which was basically a catalog of the dolls and their fashions.*

**Illustration 10.** *Fashions were not very well made and poorly packaged, in my opinion. Shown are* Cheerleader Captain *and* School Days! *The concept was brilliant and well thought out and the clothing will be judged collectible by future collectors because of the statements they make.*

with real life, except during the early 1980s when the focus was away from the teenager except for "teensploitation" as done by the media.

*Starr* and *Shaun* were unique also in that they were *Barbie* size yet had a different proportion. Clothing was not mentioned as being interchangeable. They were not listed as "friends" of *Barbie*, or even tied in at all in advertising. Springfield High was described: "Just like the high school in your town. It has a lawn where every one relaxes at lunch time. Classrooms filled with friendly faces. Sports and clubs of every kind. Dances. Pep rallies. A band. And homework, of course."

Looking backward nostalgically, my own high school was much like that. If there was unpleasantness, it was safely hidden. For myself, "Leave it to Beaver" was not so much a satire, but reality. Frankly, if I had had *Starr and Her High School Friends* at that age, I would have seen nothing out of the ordinary about them.

When I "grew up" and became a school teacher in an inner city school, I realized how very, very different life was for many. To me, knowing what I do today, I still say that a person like *Starr* is possible, and Springfield High does exist someplace, but it seems, unfortunately, to be the exception!

Along with *Starr* and *Shaun* were two girlfriends. *Starr's* best friend was *Kelley* . Her yearbook description calls her "the walking encyclopedia." "If you want to know something, ask Kelley. She reads everything, and gets straight A's in school." *Starr's* zany friend is *Tracy* . She is described as being "the star in the school plays, draws well, and plays two musical instruments." *Starr* and her friends also have a musical group. They play at the school dances and, of course, everyone loves them.

To me, therein lies the real secret to popularity. *Katy Keene* knew it, *Barbie* knew it, and *Starr* knew it. It is the undefinable ability to make those around you love your success instead of feeling threatened by it. It is admiration, not jealousy. It is the ability to, if you are a girl, have women want to be you, and men put you on a pedestal. Vice versa if you are a man.

Mattel has been very successful at creating this type of persona.

It this is true, then why was *Starr* only on the market from 1980 to 1981?

To fully understand, one has to step back from the personalities of the dolls themselves and examine the doll in a detached way. In my opinion, *Starr* was simply not pretty. Her face had a "shallow" quality and a translucence that made her look a bit "washed out." The realistic joints detracted from the beauty of the concept. The clothing was not top quality. Actually, the fantasy of the characters was the best part. Assuming not too many adults would be reading the character study on each box, it seems that the quality level AND the lack of a tie-in to *Barbie* did *Starr* in.

Now, the reader might ask, are these dolls worthy of collecting? In my opinion, any doll that makes a STATEMENT is attractive to me. *Starr and Her High School Friends*, when dressed properly and groomed meticulously (and photographed as I have done for this article), take on the personalities that Mattel intended. Under a dome, a display of these dolls

*Illustration 11. In 1980, teenagers were focused in on movies which were nicknamed "teen slaughter flicks" because a young girl and her friends were usually chased and murdered. Shown is Adrienne King in* Friday the 13th, *a Paramount release. These movies showed teens living fast life styles and dying violently!* Photograph courtesy Movie Star News, a Paramount release, 1980.

*Illustration 12. Whitman made a series of paper dolls of* Starr™. *Drawn beautifully, they captured the essence of teenage life in the early 1980s.*

*Illustration 13. The deluxe paper set was a real soda shop and schoolroom for the Springfield High bunch. Products like this add much to a collection.*

captures, for me, teenage life in the early 1980s better than a movie can, because the dolls are three-dimensional. When dolls "speak" to me about life, our culture and us as a people, I see beyond a pale face or a joint that shows. I see a slice of Americana that

I want to remember and preserve. *Starr and Her High School Friends* represent an American ideal that I hold high to this day. Hard work and determination, mixed with adventure and fun, make life an exciting journey! □

The author would like to thank Candice Irving, public relations at Mattel, for allowing Mattel trademarks to be used for educational purposes.

*Barbie*, *Ken*, *Starr*, *Shaun*, *Tracy* and *Kelley* are registered trademarks of Mattel, Inc.

*Katy Keene* is a registered trademark of Archie Comics Group, Inc.

# The 1980s — A Decade of Dolls on Review

Here we are well into the year 1990! It is hard to believe isn't it! It seems like only yesterday we were putting our disco records away, and gearing up for the 1980s. While no one can call the 1980s a quiet decade, in the doll world, the decade will be remembered most for its abundance of dolls aimed at the doll collector. Before the decade would end, many companies and many individuals would drop out, unable to compete in the high tech fast-paced world of doll collecting in the 1980s.

The decade kicked off with a resurgence of interest in the <u>FACE</u> of a doll. Most companies had skimped by the 1970s with the standard formula of just a wig and costume change to denote a new doll. The Effanbee Doll Company, in a daring move, began making celebrity dolls that actually looked like the persons they were intended to portray. The celebrity doll market was in full swing with books

(one by this author) telling of the virtues of capturing a celebrity at the peak of his/her prime in doll form. Unfortunately, many of the subjects chosen passed away during the decade. Thus one's collection took on a new and unexpected role. Added to that is the fact that some of the dolls, while excellently facially sculpted, left much to be desired in the way the body and costume looked, and with sky-high prices for substandard quality, the collectors looked elsewhere for their dolls.

It was an era when manufacturers simply did not understand the doll collectors, and in many ways, underestimated their intelligence while they kicked around phrases describing "special interest to the collector," "limited edition," "special certificate" and "one year production" dolls our way, only to see them sell for nothing at auction two years later.

As the decade moved on, some new ways to reach the consumer arose. One was the birth of the "mints," or art

organizations which sold directly to the consumer. While most of their products were of at least fair quality for the price (and actually are getting much better), the dolls were/are made in such large numbers that resale is better left to one's heirs than to attempt such in one's own lifetime.

Another wave of collecting hit the shores of the 1980s, and that was the doll artist. Famous artists were selling their molds, and now anyone could buy a kiln, and call himself/herself a "doll artist." Some were wonderful, and talent born in the 1980s has matured into some very fine artists of today. Others, lost in a maze of polyester gingham and eyelet ruffles, dropped out of sight. The reproduction artist

**Illustration 3.** *R. John Wright and his fanciful felt dolls exemplify the fine work being done by doll artists today. Good work is appreciating in value.*

**Illustration 4.** Tippi by Madame Alexander was a special doll designed for the Collectors United doll show. As a limited edition by a prestigious company, the doll will only appreciate in value in years to come.

*Illustration 5.* Rhett *and* Scarlett *by World Doll. Brilliant sculpting make celebrity dolls come to life! These are sure to hold their value. The celebrity doll craze may return this year with the dolls of the* New Kids on the Block. *The doll world is ever changing.*

that is unlike one we will ever see again. Normally sane rational people climbed over each other in a mad frenzy to get "Wilona Wetonya," or some other cleverly named doll. The collectible and play doll markets suffered greatly because of the *Cabbage Patch Kid* craze. Even the prestigious Alexander Doll Company had to resort to advertising, something it had never really had to do in the past. Eventually the craze gave way, and now the dolls are a staple, or a classic doll that still sells, but within the normal retail perimeters for a doll of its type.

As the decade moved into the latter years, more and more collectors entered the doll collecting market. **Doll Reader®** and other sources, as well as the DOTY® program brought several new groups to the collecting world. Retail shops, specializing in new dolls, catered to the collector with full selections of the spanking new baby dolls, more realistic than ever. The latest in reproduction dolls, some by local ar-

honed his/her skills also, and by the end of the decade, the word "Repro" commanded respect when well-known names were attached to that doll. Some reproduction dolls were so well done that on old bodies, with old wigs and clothes, they could defy detection in a living room cabinet. Yet as the decade progressed, and the artists grew, the reproduction doll was viewed as how a doll might look while for sale in 1880 in a Paris boutique, as artists combed the globe searching for old silks, and fabrics that looked like the French bébés would have worn over 100 years ago. The dolls actually looked like someone went back in time and brought them to the present, and thus the lowly repro doll became, in skilled hands, a hot commodity of the 1980s.

The collectible doll market was forever changed in 1983 when Xavier Roberts signed with Coleco to make the ever famous *Cabbage Patch Kid™*. The advertising claimed that no two were alike and this created a phenomenon

*Illustration 6.* A real "sleeper" that got by most collectors are the Elegante Dolls by Dakin and Faith Wick. Unbelievably lifelike, they captured doll artistry in vinyl, yet were not a commercial success. Shown are Beauty and The Beast.

tists, and the teddy bear market spilled over into the all service doll boutique, while doll artists began making limited editions for the newly emerging doll boutique customer.

This type of collector did not know of the dolls of the past, other than as a passing fancy from reading an article or two. These doll collectors did not associate with the "mainstream" collectors of the doll show circuit.

The doll shows grew in numbers quickly. Every weekend there was another show to go to...merchandise was spread too thin, and soon many shows became stagnant pools of marker-stained vinyl dolls and repro *Raggedy Anns*.

There was, however, a new group of collectors entering the market, and they were the baby boomers. Richer than any group before them, and much better educated, they were trying to find some stability in their lives. What better way than by buying the dolls they had as children. Soon those aged 25 to 45 were combing the doll shows looking for the gorgeous *Tonis*®, *Revlons*®, *Tiny Tears* and *Sweet Sue* dolls they had as children. However, those in this group wanted their dolls MINT. New expressions were coined such as "Christmas morning mint," "tissue mint," "pristine mint," all to denote that the doll had never been breathed on. Suddenly a lot of collectors who had "settled" for played-with versions of Madame Alexander and other dolls could not GIVE them away.

***Illustration 8.*** *This coy busty slightly Oriental looking fashion doll underwent many revisions and three face lifts, but she still is queen of the fashion dolls, Barbie® by Mattel. She is consistently on the best seller list and is selling better than ever!*

***Illustration 7.*** *Mary Hartline by Ideal exemplifies the all hard plastic doll mint-in-the-box that is so sought after today by collectors. A doll in this condition might bring several hundred dollars while a played-with version would bring less than $75.*

The new collector wanted perfection and was willing and able to pay for it. Price guides were very misused, and the truth was (and still is) that nothing is selling but junk at low prices, and mint rare dolls at high prices. There is no market at the present for the played-with doll unless priced at a fraction of book value.

Adding to the thrill of the decade was the celebration of some very important events. In 1989, *Barbie*®, who in the past 30 years had become a living legend, celebrated her 30th anniversary with a special doll for the press. Ironically, that will be the *Barbie* collectible of all time. Now in ethnic versions, *Barbie* represents all women of every race.

Two entertainment milestones, *Gone With the Wind* and *The Wizard of Oz*, also celebrated 50th anniversaries with lots of good and some not so good collectibles.

***Illustration 9.*** *Barbie® as seen in Japan. Now available with the delicate coloring of the Northern Europeans, or shown here as an exaggeration of the American Dream, the 1980s brought new faces to many classic dolls.*

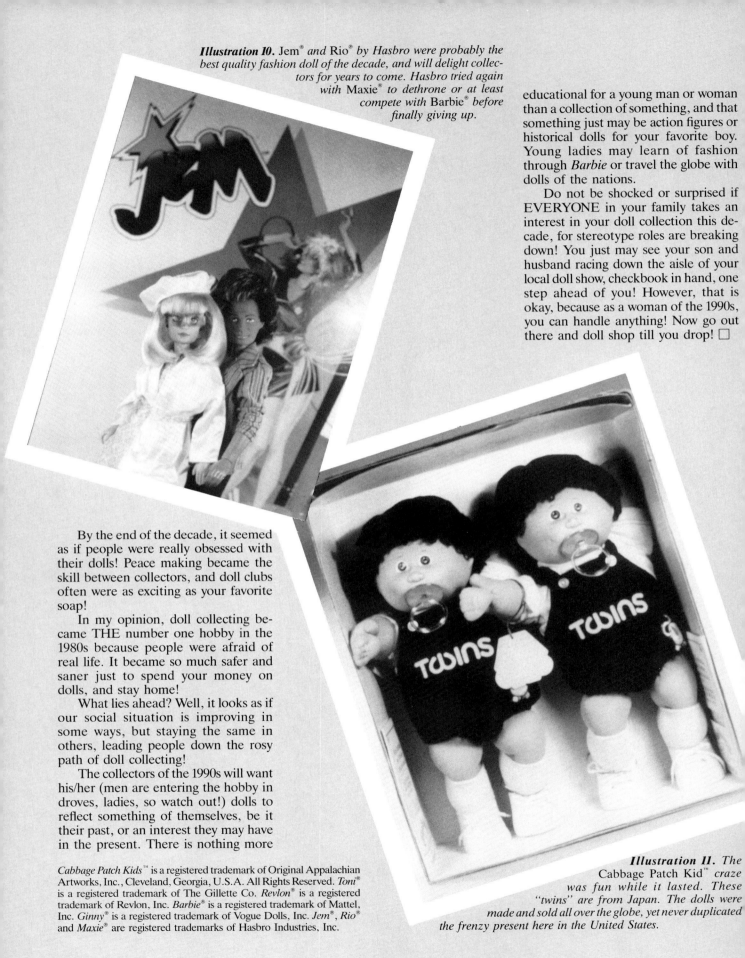

**Illustration 10.** Jem® and Rio® by Hasbro were probably the best quality fashion doll of the decade, and will delight collectors for years to come. Hasbro tried again with Maxie® to dethrone or at least compete with Barbie® before finally giving up.

educational for a young man or woman than a collection of something, and that something just may be action figures or historical dolls for your favorite boy. Young ladies may learn of fashion through *Barbie* or travel the globe with dolls of the nations.

Do not be shocked or surprised if EVERYONE in your family takes an interest in your doll collection this decade, for stereotype roles are breaking down! You just may see your son and husband racing down the aisle of your local doll show, checkbook in hand, one step ahead of you! However, that is okay, because as a woman of the 1990s, you can handle anything! Now go out there and doll shop till you drop! □

By the end of the decade, it seemed as if people were really obsessed with their dolls! Peace making became the skill between collectors, and doll clubs often were as exciting as your favorite soap!

In my opinion, doll collecting became THE number one hobby in the 1980s because people were afraid of real life. It became so much safer and saner just to spend your money on dolls, and stay home!

What lies ahead? Well, it looks as if our social situation is improving in some ways, but staying the same in others, leading people down the rosy path of doll collecting!

The collectors of the 1990s will want his/her (men are entering the hobby in droves, ladies, so watch out!) dolls to reflect something of themselves, be it their past, or an interest they may have in the present. There is nothing more

**Illustration 11.** *The Cabbage Patch Kid*™ *craze was fun while it lasted. These "twins" are from Japan. The dolls were made and sold all over the globe, yet never duplicated the frenzy present here in the United States.*

# Kimberly®...
# A Play Doll Turns Collectible

Many times I receive letters addressed to my column "Dollars and Doll Sense," lamenting the fact that good quality dolls of children are all priced out of reach of many collectors. The devaluation of the dollar has, in some cases, more than doubled the price of the lovely imported children such as those by Heidi Ott, Goetz, Zapf and Corolle. With the *Sasha* dolls out of production AND out of sight price wise, the less than affluent collector or the collector just not interested enough in this genre of dolls is left out in the cold!

Well, in our not so distant past, a lovely doll, of impeccable quality and superior design, crept right past us all. In the antique business, that phenomenon is commonly called a "sleeper," a term to mean that otherwise watchful collectors, dealers and investors were "asleep" at the helm, and a good buy slipped right by them.

In this case, that incredible buy may still be found, with some dilligent searching, right in your local area, possibly on sale at half price or more! That doll is *Kimberly*, in my opinion, the quintessential child doll NOT aimed at the doll collector, but not promoted to the child, either, and therefore doomed to a rapid demise.

At Toy Fair, in the early 1980s, doll collecting and doll collectors were just being noticed. The incredible rise (and eventual fall) of collectible dolls such as those by Madame Alexander, Effanbee

and others, was being carefully analyzed by marketing experts who could not understand why collectors would pay $50 for a doll dress made 30 years ago and showing some wear, yet would not plop down $5.00 for a new garment! Auction reports, magazine articles and other sources told toy manufacturers that collectors obviously had money to spend and WANTED to spend it. If they could just find a way to get the collector to spend it on NEW dolls, the pie could be theirs.

Thus began in earnest the race for the collector's DOLLars, a madcap, often now incredible competition to stop the collector from spending money on old dolls and spend it on current dolls.

In all fairness, much of this frenzy of activity was beneficial to the collector. Today's marketplace, after an enormous shakedown, is stronger than ever. Many doll artists and a few mass manufacturers DID figure out what the collector wanted and delivered it.

◊

***OPPOSITE PAGE: Illustration 1.*** Kimberly *by Tomy, produced in 1981, was a top quality child doll 17in (43cm) tall which had features present on dolls costing five times more! She was discontinued in 1985!*

***RIGHT: Illustration 2.*** *Patsy Pease, star of the NBC Soap "Days of Our Lives," plays Kimberly Brady, and looks astonishing like the* Kimberly *doll. Perhaps a tie-in existed? NBC publicity photograph.*

For children, the years of the early 1980s were most trying. In my humble opinion, the child of today, perhaps lacking the strong guidance of family, church, home and school, is unduly influenced by television and peer pressure. In order for a doll to succeed, it must pass the "Saturday Morning Line," or, in other words, the toy must be rammed down the throats of a child 20 times a day on television. Next, all their friends must want the doll. IF these requirements are met, then the doll stands a chance of perhaps being a success.

The Tomy Corporation, in 1981 at Toy Fair, showed a lovely 17in (43cm) doll of impeccable quality. Without getting overly technical, the doll was of European quality, with features not seen here in decades! She had a five-piece rotational molded body, (rotational molding means that the pieces are constantly rotated to avoid seams), a "strung" body construction and nylon rooted hair that was the quality of the *Toni®* dolls made by Ideal in the early 1950s! The hair was so luxurious that it could be set, parted and restyled. It had been decades since dolls had hair that wonderful. Adding to this, the facial mold itself was lovely, with lifelike painted eyes that sparkled with life. She was at least as pretty as ALL the expensive collectors' dolls costing HUNDREDS more, yet she was aimed at children and meant to retail for $20!

I remember at Toy Fair that year commenting to the tour guide at Tomy that frankly the doll was marketed all wrong. It seemed more like a collectors' doll than a doll for a child, or at least there should be some crossover advertising, but no one seemed to be listening.

**ABOVE LEFT: Illustration 3.** Kimberly *(whose hair is styled by the author, as is the hair on all the dolls photographed) wears the look of a schoolgirl in this charming outfit complete with clog shoes, notebook, comb and pencil in her school bag!*

**LEFT: Illustration 4.** Gettin' Fancy Kimberly *with a new smile face and side-parted hair goes ice skating in a fabulous outfit complete with metal-bladed lace-up skates.*

That Christmas, the doll appeared in gorgeous outfits, well thought out, AND a black version of the doll was also available, that while pretty, was really just the white doll dipped in black paint. It had no ethnic quality at all. Extra boxed outfits were available as well, with athletic and party themes.

In my neighborhood, (my "test" market), the little girls loved *Kimberly* and could be seen fussing with the hair on the front steps. Many mothers compared her to the *Sasha* dolls and commented on how good the quality was for the price.

Now one might ask, with all this going for it, why did *Kimberly* fail? Well, several factors already mentioned must be taken into account. Television advertising was weak on the doll, but for the first year *Kimberly* held her own. Finally in 1984 an open-mouth version with a part in the hair called *Gettin' Fancy Kimberly*, was introduced. A beautiful doll, she had all the markings of success. Unfortunately, the almost mystical, now defunct, but legendary *Cabbage Patch Kids*™ by Coleco, had arrived the previous year, and like a plague of locusts, devoured all other dolls' chances of success. Another entire article could be written by this author about that crazy time when I watched my next-door neighbor (who had two small girls) sleep overnight in her car to be first in line in below-freezing weather to win the "right" to purchase two dolls. (We are talking about someone who would not stand in line five minutes to be waited on in the deli department of the supermarket, so you can get a better idea of the phenomenon!)

**ABOVE RIGHT: Illustration 5.** *Black version of* Gettin' Fancy Kimberly *featured hair play as the main theme.*

**RIGHT: Illustration 6.** *Another black version of the standard doll in nightshirt with sleeping bag, showing the long straight hair the doll comes with before restyling.*

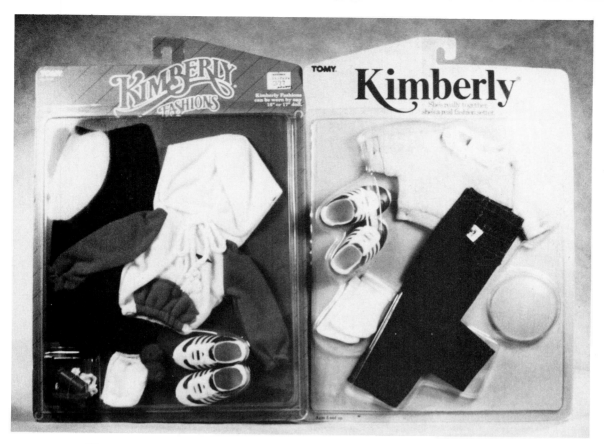

*Illustration 7. Extra carded outfits featured athletic themes with realistic accessories.*

The *Cabbage Patch Kid* mystique is something that comes along only once! It greatly influenced the doll marketplace for several years, and things are just starting to get back to normal!

*Kimberly* went wrong because she was aimed at children who did not appreciate her once the *Cabbage Patch Kid* craze hit, and adult collectors did not even know about her! Thus, she fits the definition of a true "sleeper," or a doll that got by us all!

The story of *Kimberly* proves just how fascinating the doll marketplace is, and how "fickle" the tastes of children and collectors can be. *Kimberly* also teaches us that no matter what your doll collecting budget (or even if price is no object) that good quality dolls every so often get produced and quickly disappear unless we are watchful! You CAN have quality dolls for little money...all it takes is a keen eye, gas in the car and an afternoon to go exploring. There just may be another doll like *Kimberly* out there waiting for you to find her! □

*Illustration 8. The packaging of* Gettin' Fancy Kimberly. *The doll was a high quality product, but was marketed for children who only had eyes for* Cabbage Patch Kids™! *Many adult collectors did not even know* Kimberly *existed!*

# Black Fashion Dolls of the 1970s and 1980s

"Black is Beautiful" as the saying goes, and the panorama of ethnically correct dolls on the market today certainly proves that point. Today, a child that is black, Hispanic, Asian or white can have a doll, such as Mattel's *Barbie*®, in his/her own race, and thus have a role model that helps build self-esteem. This, however, was not always the case.

Before we can intelligently discuss the current wave of ethnic dolls, it is necessary to look at the past few decades of black collectible dolls.

In the 1950s, the socio-economic portrait of the average black family was not the rosy picture of post-war prosperity that whites enjoyed. This author can vividly remember attending the Jamestown, Virginia, festival when Queen Elizabeth of England visited in 1957. I was shocked as a child to see that there were separate bathrooms and even water fountains clearly labeled "colored" and "white." Living in the North, I had never seen this, and it was a chilling reminder that discrimination was far from over.

Several leading companies did offer black dolls for those families who could afford them. Two of most notable were *Cynthia*, a *Margaret*-faced Alexander doll simply painted with dark paint, and Vogue's *Ginny*®, which was actually black hard plastic. These dolls today command much money. (*Cynthia* is about $500 up in mint condition and a black *Ginny* can be $1500 up when mint!)

There were some black baby dolls, the best being Ideal's *Sara Lee*, and others by lesser known manufacturers. Segregation was still very evident, and it was not limited to blacks.

While one looks back at the 1950s with rose-colored

glasses, the reality was that Jews, Italians, those of Polish descent with unpronounceable names, Catholics and just about everybody else that was not a WASP (White Anglo-Saxon Protestant) strived to be part of the mainstream.

Even the top singers of the day "Anglicized" their names. Robert Riderelli became Bobby Rydell. Conchetta Francioso was renamed Connie Francis. Frankie Avaloni was — well

*Illustration 2. Superstar Diana Ross has had a successful career. Today, lovelier than ever, she is indeed a role model to emulate.* Photograph courtesy of Movie Star News.

*Illustration 1. This incredible likeness of Diana Ross was made in the late 1970s. It was the second time the celebrity and singer had been captured in doll form.*

*Illustration 3. The packaging of the Mego doll featured a portrait of Miss Ross, daring to put it right next to the doll so buyers could see just how good a likeness it was!*

115

you get the point. Blacks were especially hard hit because while an Italian could pass for a WASP with a doctored name and some genteel clothing, those of color could not.

Added to this was the fact that the more "white" black people could make themselves during the 1950s, the more chances they had at success. It is no wonder that blacks often gave their children white dolls and that often black dolls were rejected, even by black children.

Proof of this is evident when, in 1967, Mattel issued *Barbie's MODern Cousin, Francie*® in a black version. (For an illustration of this rare doll, see "*Francie*®...*Barbie's MODern*

*Cousin*" by this author in the November 1990 issue of **Doll Reader**®, pages 152 to 156.) While it was theoretically possible for *Barbie* to have a black cousin, Mattel had issued her first in white the year before. Black children loved and adored *Barbie*, and to them she was a blonde goddess who was a piece of the American Dream they could own. A black version of *Francie* was not welcomed, even by blacks themselves.

The early 1960s also produced some versions of white dolls "dipped" in black (in other words, the same mold was used, only with black vinyl). American Character's *Tressy*® and Ideal's *Tammy*® both were

on the market a short time in black. Also, at Toy Fair in 1964, Mattel had shown a black version of *Skipper*®, *Barbie's Little Sister*, a concept that, in my opinion, was ludicrous.

A huge breakthrough came in 1969 when Mattel issued *Julia*, based on Diahann Carroll's role on the television show of the same name. This was a huge success because blacks saw *Julia* as the first mainstream role model. The television series featured Miss Carroll as a nurse, making a good income, having a child and being respected. Blacks loved the show because, for the first time ever, a black woman had a television series where she was not a maid.

Another black doll introduced in 1968 was *Christie*®, *Barbie's Friend*. This was quite a racial breakthrough that is often overlooked. Here was the Queen of the WASPS, *Barbie*, having a black girlfriend. Black leaders and, more importantly, black children, saw this as a wonderful idea. Now, as Mattel television commercials showed, a *Barbie* party at a girl's house, or a meeting of the *Barbie* Fan Club, could include black children as well who now had their own friend to bring along. Still, in the back of their minds, *Barbie* herself was white, and was still Queen of the Prom, while her black friends were merely

**Illustration 4.** Superstar Christie®, *from the late 1970s, while dressed in yellow instead of pink like the white version, was still just the white doll painted black.*

**Illustration 5.** Fun to Dress Barbie®, *from the late 1980s, used a new ethnic mold. Modeling an Oscar de la Renta gown, she is indeed stunning.*

**Illustration 6.** *The year 1989 saw the introduction of* Flo Jo, *a doll based on Florence Joyce Gainer, a popular athletic star. While an excellent likeness, like most others (if not all others), it could not compete with* Barbie.

"accessories" to her life. Nevertheless, it was a start.

In my personal life, I was a junior high school Spanish and French teacher in the mid 1970s. The school I was in was all black. This gave me quite a glimpse of a lifestyle with which I had never had contact. Many of the concepts presented here and in my book, *Doll Fashion Anthology and Price Guide*, published by Hobby House Press, Inc., are based on five years of working with black students and their families. Few realize how little self-esteem these children had during this period, and Mattel was at the forefront in the 1980s of those trying to correct the problem.

The first real breakthrough came in 1980 when Mattel issued *Black Barbie*®. Trading off slogans used on the television show "Good Times," featuring a black ghetto family, this

**Illustration 7.** *In 1988, the Olmec Corporation issued* Naomi *and billed her as the first doll not just painted white. Her beaded "cornrow" hair style added to the ethnic correctness of the doll.*

new *Barbie* had an Afro (or natural) hairdo, instead of processed straight hair. The box stated she was "dynamite," a slogan used by JJ on "Good Times." Even her dress was something flashy, and she came with a hair pick for her Afro.

The doll sold quite well, and many blacks thought this was a dream come true. Now a child who adored *Barbie* could at last

**Illustration 8.** *A close-up of the new ethnic mold used by Mattel for* Barbie. *The clothing and jewelry are by Mattel.*

**Illustration 9.** Black Barbie *and* Skipper *make a fabulous duo. The outfits and the dolls are charming.*

**Illustration 10.** *In 1980,* Black Barbie *was introduced followed by a black* Ken® *who sported the then popular Afro hair style.*

**Illustration 11.** Ken *has not been overlooked by Mattel, for he comes with the new short hair seen on black men today as well as a mustache! Wardrobes for the dolls look wonderful on the black versions.*

project her own identity on the doll the way Mattel intended white girls to do with *Barbie*. Still, while a breakthrough, she still was a white doll mold "dipped" in brown vinyl.

Another breakthrough came that same year when Mattel innocently issued *Magic Curl Barbie®*. This doll featured hair that could be straightened and curled. Also issued was a black version of the doll, BUT there was no mention on the box about her being black. The packing merely substituted black photographs for the white ones, and both dolls were coifed and dressed the same. This gave the black version of *Barbie* equal status.

The final breakthrough occurred when *California*

*Christie®*, with an ethnic mold (black facial features), became part of the Mattel line in the late 1980s. This doll's mold has now been used almost exclusively to make the black versions of *Barbie* seen on the market.

Last in the Mattel saga, *Happy Holidays Barbie®* for 1990, was issued for the first time since the series began in 1988 in a black version using the new ethnic mold. Even Sears' exclusive *Lavender Surprise Barbie®* came in both black and white. At last black children's needs were being met.

To come full circle, in 1989, Mattel finally did issue *Barbie's Little Sister, Skipper®* in a black version, which black children love dearly. In addition, *Essence* magazine, a publication for upscale blacks, featured an ad with a black child playing with a black doll. Mattel deserves a real "thumbs up" for being responsible as a leader in civil rights. As a former teacher, I cannot tell you the impact that toys have on children. Now, values can be taught, not only with *Barbie*, but with some of the other fantastic black dolls available.

There have been other black fashion dolls over the years, that are worthy of mention.

In the late 1960s, Ideal issued a *Diana Ross* doll featuring Miss Ross as part of the Supremes. This doll used the *Crissy* mold and sported an Afro hairdo and gold gown. Miss Ross reportedly received $10,000 for the rights to her name.

In the late 1970s, Mego issued a fantastic likeness of Miss Ross in a 12in (31cm) size, elaborately packed and dressed, for which Miss Ross allegedly received one million dollars for the use of her name! The doll is held in high regard by collectors, Diana Ross fans and black children, among others.

In 1988, the Olmec corporation issued *Naomi* and billed her in its press release as "not just a white face painted black." While not, in my opinion, the quality of Mattel dolls, she did fulfill her promise and did look quite ethnic. Recently the same doll, now named *Elesse*, could be found in toy stores.

The year 1989 saw the release of *Flo Jo* (Florence Joyce Gainer, the athlete) which was an excellent likeness of the celebrity, but for some reason, the doll did not sell well, at least in the Philadelphia area, for they were marked down. Her wardrobe was very nicely made and featured a variety of fashions for all occasions. Probably *Barbie* was just too much to compete with!

Sometimes collectors, especially those without children, tend to place their own views on dolls, but you would be amazed the impact toys have on children. Not only did I witness this while teaching, today I see many collectors harbor great bitterness and anger (especially some male collectors) over not having received a particular doll. Many women and men can describe in vivid detail what they did not receive as a child. Imagine, if you can, what a black child must have felt like. Many did not have the means to buy black dolls, and when they did, they realized they were just the white doll painted black.

In my opinion, some of the social problems we have today in our inner cities can be traced to low self-esteem that has its roots in playthings.

At least in dolls, blacks and other minorities are

**Illustration 12.** *The 1989* Unicef Barbie® *came in a wonderful black version.*

**Illustration 13.** *In 1990,* Black Barbie *has really come into her own as an airline pilot! Imagine, when* Barbie *was created, she was only a stewardess and a nurse (which is all fine if not forced on you because of your gender!), while today she is a pilot, flying high for civil rights!*

becoming a leading subject in manufacturing, and the blacks I speak with at doll shows and clubs seemed pleased with the trends started in the 1980s. As the saying goes, "Black is Beautiful," and that certainly is true in the doll world of the 1990s. □

*Barbie®; Barbie's MODern Cousin, Francie®; Francie®; Skipper®, Barbie's Little Sister; Julia®; Christie®, Barbie's Friend; Black Barbie®; Magic Curl Barbie®; California Christie®; Happy Holidays Barbie®; Lavender Surprise Barbie®; Superstar Christie®; Fun To Dress Barbie®; Ken®; Animal Lovin' Barbie®; Animal Lovin' Ken and Unicef Barbie® are registered trademarks of Mattel, Inc.*
*Ginny® is a registered trademark of Vogue Dolls, Inc.*
*Tressy® is a registered trademark of the American Character Doll Co.*
*Tammy® is a registered trademark of the Ideal Toy Corp.*

**Illustration 14.** *I am surprised that this got by the press! On the back of the box of the black* Animal Lovin' Barbie®, *the black doll is shown with the white* Ken, *making an interracial couple! This was because there was no black* Animal Lovin' Ken®.

**Illustration 15.** *In 1969, Mattel issued* Julia, *based on Diahann Carroll's role as a television nurse. The show portrayed a black woman as a professional.*

# CHER®...
## A "Sing"ular Sensation

Glamorous, outrageous, sexy and bizarre, these are just a few terms quite often used when describing a tall raven-haired half Indian/Armenian, female singer known as Cherilyn Sarkisian LaPierre Bono Allman, or simply Cher!

She was born Cherilyn Sarkisian LaPierre on May 20, 1946, in El Centro, California. Cher grew up in Hollywood, where her mother was an actress, and studied acting and singing as a youngster. She dropped out of school and left home at 16 in pursuit of her "big break."

That break came during 1962, in a Hollywood coffee shop, where a 16-year-old Cher was "spotted" by a short 27-year-old Italian with a Prince Valiant haircut known as Sonny Bono. Sonny had been working in the record industry for several years and upon seeing Cher, brought her along to sing background vocals for his employer, record whiz producer Phil Spector.

Cher found a home at the legendary Gold Star Recording Studios in Hollywood as a background vocalist, singing "oohs" and "aahs" for the Crystals and the Ronettes.

Sonny took Cher in and, after he ended his relationship with Phil Spector in early 1964, slowly began molding her for stardom. The first step was creating their own act. The two donned Egyptian costumes, christened themselves "Caesar and Cleo," and found no work. The team quickly switched to "Sonny and Cher" and in 1965 came up with their legendary hit recording, Sonny's composition "I Got You Babe."

***Illustration 2.*** *Here* Cher *radiates her glamour queen image dressed in* Radiant. *The sequins and feathers were just a few of the many Cher trademarks along with her signature long straight hair, eyelashes and fingernails!*

**Illustration 3.** Growing Hair Cher, *the second version of the* Cher *doll, incorporated the "Cleopatra-like" look Cher showed frequently on "The Sonny and Cher Show." The resemblance between the doll and real-life celebrity is astounding!*

Long haired, clad in beads and bell-bottoms, Sonny and Cher quickly became the perfect replica of the 1960s hippie as well as major stars. Cher turned her entire life over to Sonny and he made her a star by his gimmickry and Svengali approach. As Cher stated: "He controlled the whole situation. He booked the gigs and managed every phase of the work." (J. Randy Taraborrelli, *Cher*, St. Martins Press, 1986.)

The duo had a string of hit records,

**Illustration 4.** Cher *recaptures the pose, costume and look that landed her the cover of* Time *magazine in March of 1975,* La Plume, *the outfit, was designed by Bob Mackie, as were all of the doll's ensembles, and paid homage to his original beaded feathered dress that Cher wore on the magazine cover and made famous.*

***Illustration 5.*** *A publicity shot of Sonny and Cher in their "Beat Goes On" days. Long haired, clad in boots and bell-bottoms, the two became perfect replicas of the 1960s hippies as well as major stars. Note how coincidentally the couple is shown tug of war like, much how their future married relationship was like. The two were always on opposite ends, with Sonny playing the part of dictator.* Photograph by Movie Star News.

like "The Beat Goes On" and "What Now My Love," television appearances on "Hullabaloo" and "Shindig," and two flop movies, *Good Times* and *Chastity*, that exploited 1960s youth themes - love and peace. Sonny and Cher represented "The Love Generation," acting as if they were married, when they were not. The two were living together and had that been revealed, their innocent pop image would have been shattered.

It was not until shortly before the birth of their daughter, Chastity, in 1969, that Sonny and Cher were married. The decade was over and ahead lay a yellow brick road filled with many potholes.

For the new decade, Sonny radically re-created Cher from 1960s hippie to 1970s glamour girl. This transition was apparent in 1971 when the team landed their own CBS variety show, which began as a summer replacement and turned into a major regular season hit. "The Sonny and Cher Comedy Hour" saw the couple, with a glossier image, taking pot shots at each other during the opening of each show.

The series showcased Cher who sang of gypsies, tramps and thieves, of dark ladies and half-breeds all, of course, dressed in the most risqué Bob Mackie costumes, for which she became famous. Gone forever were the bell-bottoms, fur vests and leather boots. "Television was so damn drab," Cher said, "and that's the only reason I wanted to dress up." (J. Randy Taraborrelli, *Cher*, St. Martins Press, 1986.) Dress up she did, from the television screen to the record charts with such hits as "Gypsies, Tramps and Thieves," "The Way of Love," "Half-Breed" and "Dark Lady."

At 26, Cher was a television superstar and it was her mystique and charisma that carried the couple's show and eventually eclipsed that of her partner. "I'm kind of like Queen of a mediocre medium," she said. "Television is the kind of thing you can pay attention to if you wish, and if you don't, you can go clean out your drawers."

It was during the run of their television show that Sonny and Cher's marital problems became public knowledge. The main problem is that Cher finally realized she had surrendered not only the controlling of her career to Sonny, but her personal life as well. "If you watched 'The Sonny and Cher Comedy Hour,' you assumed I was this

***Illustration 6.*** *Roll the cameras! The* Sonny *and* Cher *dolls are dressed to match as they often were on their television show.* Sonny *sports his* White Tux *while* Cher *models* Radiant. *Bob Mackie designed all of the couple's costumes for their television show, but only* Cher's *not* Sonny's *doll wardrobe.*

wisecracking girl who ran our lives offstage, 'cause Sonny seemed so meek and easy going," she told *Cosmopolitan* magazine. "Hah! In real life he was this Sicilian dictator husband - I could say nothing! We were in the Nielsen top ten, we had all this money, everybody told me how lucky and happy I was - when actually I weighed ninety-three pounds, I was constantly sick, could not eat, could not sleep. I got suicidal. And I thought, either I'm going to leave

Sonny, or I am going to jump out the window."

In 1974 the "Sonny and Cher Comedy Hour" ended when the couple divorced. Cher was now "freed," her life a clean slate, and she was ready for the creation of something new - a solo variety series and, yes, another marriage! Her self-titled television show, "Cher," with an emphasis on music, debuted on CBS in February of 1975. Three days after she divorced Sonny, Cher married

Greg Allman, leader of the Allman Brothers band and a self-proclaimed heroin addict. It was a stormy union, although it survived Cher's filing for divorce nine days after the marriage. The "Cher" show took a nosedive in the ratings after she married Allman, and came to an abrupt end in early January of 1976.

A month later, a pregnant Cher reunited - professionally at least, with her ex-husband, Sonny, and starred in a revived variety series on CBS titled "The Sonny and Cher Show." Capitalizing on their reunion, the Mego Corp. issued in 1976 the *Sonny* and *Cher* celebrity/fashion dolls. These vinyl dolls were of high quality and really looked like the real-life couple.

Although the dolls came with some matching fashions like *Space Prince* and *Princess*, it was the *Cher* doll, complete with luxurious long hair and Bob Mackie designed wardrobe, that was the real attraction! The *Cher* wardrobe included the star's signature flashy exotic costumes such as *Electric Feathers, Pink Fluff, Radiant* and *Madame Chan.* Cher's part Indian background was conveyed in such ensembles as *Indian Squaw,* ala "Half-Breed," *Cherokee* and the *Cher Dressing Room* play setting, which came complete with Indian art!

Perhaps the most famous and collectible *Cher* outfits are *Laverne* and *La Plume.* The *Laverne* costume was a direct likeness to the one Cher wore on television when performing the memorable gossipy character in leopard-print body stocking and oddball glasses, with the nagging whining cackle of a voice. The *La Plume* ensemble pays homage to the beaded dress that made the cover of *Time* in 1975, the most controversial and famous. People still talk about it! The cover was magnificent and showed

*ABOVE LEFT: Illustration 9.* Cher *assumes the role of Dragon Lady wearing, appropriately, the* Dragon Lady *costume from her wardrobe. This red and gold satin ensemble is one of the more beautiful* Cher *outfits and clearly capitalizes on the theme of "costume dressing."*

*ABOVE RIGHT: Illustration 10. Of course, a television glamour queen has to keep her wardrobe somewhere and the* Cher *doll kept hers in her own travel trunk, shown here with the box. The trunk came with travel stickers for application, from, one would assume, places where Cher visited and performed.*

Cher, deeply tanned, wearing a Mackie see-through gown, with silver bugle bead trim and white feathers. This cover clearly personified Cher's 1970s persona - that of television glamour girl.

The *Cher* doll stood 12¼in (31cm) with long rooted hair and eyelashes and came in three different versions. The first was dressed in a basic pink halter gown, nothing glamorous, which is what one would expect. The second version was *Growing Hair Cher* that had bangs and a key wind to make the hair shorter. When short, the hair resembled a Cleopatra-like style that Cher wore occasionally, as a wig, on the television show. The growing hair doll's dress differed from that of the "original" in that it was glittering black and white. In essence, a little more "Cher." A third, a 12in (31cm) version, was is-

sued in 1981 and was very cheaply made. The rooting of the hair was extremely thin and the costume was nothing more than a shabby one-piece swimsuit! One interesting note is the fact that the "original" version's box lacked a photograph of Cher on it, which was on the other two.

Sonny and Cher tried opening their new show with the same put-downs that had marked their earlier successful series, but as a divorced couple it just was not as enjoyable as the original and was canceled at the end of the 1976 to 1977 season. "I guess the whole affair was pretty amazing," Cher recalled a couple of years later. "I don't think anyone had ever done this. I went back to a man I had been divorced from, and I was pregnant by another man who had been divorcing me. All of America watched it unfold on TV. In the history

of this country, that's probably never happened." (J. Randy Taraborrelli, *Cher*, St. Martins Press, 1986.)

Cher found that along with the demise of "The Sonny and Cher Show," her marriage to Greg Allman dissolved. The only positive addition was their son, Elijah Blue. Cher was no longer a prime time regular, a hit recording artist or a wife. She was once again solo and legally changed her name to Cher. "I didn't like either one of my husbands," Cher says, "Why carry their names around? I don't want to be identified as Mrs. anybody." Through the years she's been romantically linked with Gene Simmons of Kiss and rock musician Les Dudek, with whom she formed a rock band called Black Rose. The group had one album which bombed and then disbanded.

**Illustration 11.** *A mint-in-box* Growing Hair Cher. *This was the first box that showed a photograph of the real Cher on its cover. The 1981 version of the doll also showed a photograph of the celebrity which differed from the one shown here.*

**Illustration 12.** *A* Growing Hair Cher *modeling* Pink Fluff, *a beautiful white gown with a pink see-through over cape complete with feather trim.*

Throughout the 1980s, Cher has been most visible as an actress. It was a seed that took a decade to germinate and is now being noticed by everyone. Starring in such films as *Come Back to the 5 and Dime, Jimmy Dean, Jimmy Dean* (she made her Broadway debut in the play), *Silkwood*, for which she received an Oscar nomination for Best Supporting Actress, the Oscar-robbed nominated *Mask, The Witches of Eastwick*, the courtroom thriller *Suspect* and the 1987 comedy *Moonstruck* for which she won the Academy Award for Best Actress. Cher has come full circle and found happiness. "I like what I'm doing now, but I'm not sure which part I like," she says. Two years ago Cher returned to the recording studios, after a six year hiatus, for her musical comeback. The album, simply titled "Cher," netted two Top Ten singles and heard Cher stronger and never more comfortable, the reason being that she masterminded the album and was in control for the first time. She even directed her own video to one of the songs! Late last year Cher debuted her own signature perfume aptly titled "Uninhibited."

For more than two decades, Cher has shown that she is a survivor in an entertainment business notorious for its fads and has-beens, her secret being that she has consistently changed with the times. From flower child singer of the 1960s, a glamour queen of television and nightclubs of the 1970s, to a successful actress and independent mother in the 1980s, Cher is truly a singular sensation!

*Illustration 13.* Cher today, looking back at her career as a 1960s flower child singer, a 1970s television glamour queen and 1980s accomplished actress. She has truly come full circle and looks ahead to what the 1990s will bring. Photograph by Movie Star News.

# Rare and Unusual Collectible Dolls

Every day the collector of modern and collectible dolls is bombarded with examples of mass-manufactured dolls. Most, if not nearly all, of these dolls are in played-with condition and are, at best, common types of dolls.

You know the types of dolls of which I speak...the Madame Alexander dolls with pale faces and badly laundered clothing, sporting replaced shoes and socks; the *Barbie*® dolls with lip paint missing, ponytails down and fingers chewed; the "doll artist" or reproduction doll that has slash marks for eyebrows and layers and layers of out-of-scale fabrics and lace!

Yes, it is a confusing market of items from which to choose and the collector who loves dolls is forced to take space and money into consideration with each purchase.

The nice part of all this is that because there are so many dolls from which to choose, the collector can decide in just which direction to proceed. Some collectors love the played-with dolls and take delight in restoring them to near mint condition. This is a wonder-

*Illustration 2. This unbelievable Dewees Cochran Portrait Doll was made in the late 1930s and came in her original box. Her tag says her name is* Gloria Ann *and she sports a greyhound pin on her coat. The doll is all composition with a human hair wig and sleep eyes.*

**LEFT: Illustration 1.** *This one-of-a-kind mint-in-the-box* Shirley Temple *doll dates from 1939 and is the most mint doll I have ever seen. She is dressed in an outfit from the movie* The Bluebird. Marge Meisinger Collection.

*Illustration 3.* Most Raynal dolls are cloth, but this doll is all celluloid with flirty eyes and came with paper tags and a metal Raynal pin. She stumped even the most astute antique doll collectors and won a blue ribbon at a UFDC convention.

*Illustration 5. This is a simple rag doll bought for $10.00 at a show, BUT it turns out she is a rare Fisher-girl made by the Annalee Doll Company in the 1950s and worth at least $400! Would you recognize this?*

*Illustration 4. Most collectors would pass this doll by as a Deanna Durbin doll. The educated collector would realize that her backwards "21" marking and button saying she is a Judy Garland doll make her a rare and unusual doll of the star as a teenager.*

ful practice unless the doll, in played-with condition, is priced at near mint value (unfortunately a common practice). Other collectors, with minds towards perfectionism and investment, choose dolls that are common, yet mint-in-the-box, such as *Toni®, Sweet Sue,*

*Revlon®* and other 1950s treasures. Whether these dolls will increase in value is relatively uncertain. Mint examples of collectible dolls have been increasing at about 20 percent a year and, in the case of *Barbie* collectibles, a 50 percent to 100 percent a year growth

pattern is seen with no end in sight!

There is yet another category of doll that is out there to collect and that is the rare and unusual collectible doll. Many people are afraid of this type of doll for there is no "set" value on the price. Collectors who claim they collect for fun, often overspend the family budget and like to be assured that if emergencies arose, their doll collections would bail them out. Well, that, ladies and gentlemen, may or may not be the case, for doll collections are not designed for instant liquidation in an emergency situation. It takes time to find a buyer willing to pay "book" price or somewhere near it.

What makes rare and unusual collectible dolls such treasures is the thrill that you own something unique...something not seen every day. Yet, with this thrill comes the reality that not everyone may be interested in a rare version of a common doll at a premium price. To many, this adds to the fun, sort of like parachute jumping. You are taking a chance, a gamble as it were, that not everyone may desire your extraordinary example of a doll.

On the bright side, however, is the fact that over the past 20 years collectible dolls have gained acceptance at UFDC (United Federation of Doll Clubs, Inc.) conventions, while the rare and unusual have commanded high prices. Sometimes these prices are three to four times the price of the same

doll in an easy-to-find version.

An example of this would be a stunning dark blue satin ball gown for *Barbie* which Mattel issued in the mid 1960s. It was floor length with an overcoat that had a fur collar

*Illustration 7. Is this just another* Toni *doll? No, this is* Sara Ann, *an euphemism for Saran, a synthetic hair fiber used on the same doll, MINUS the expensive Gillette license fee! This rare doll is a knockoff by the same company!*

*Illustration 6. Madame Alexander made* So-Lite *babies in the 1930s to 1940s. Most were white, so this rare black version is indeed a treasure. The doll, like all of Madame's cloth dolls, is unmarked but the clothing is labeled. Found nude, this could escape being spotted for the rare treasure she is. Ann Tardie Collection.*

***Illustration 8.*** *Every doll collector recognizes Ideal's* Patty Playpal. *However, these dolls are only 16in (41cm) tall instead of 36in (91cm). Called* Petite Patty, *they are extremely rare and worth about $250 up each.* Colleen Giles Collection.

and was called "Midnight Blue." Today, in mint condition with all accessories, it commands a price of about $250. Just recently it has come to light that Mattel made the same outfit for the European market in a beautiful shade of pink. The value? As yet no established price exists, which adds to the mystery, for some collectors are not interested in something made for Europe as they are col-

***Illustration 9.*** *When* Barbie *arrived in 1959, every company put out a similar doll. One of the most unusual and rare in the box dolls is this* Miss Seventeen...A Beauty Queen *made by Marx. Like the German Bild* Lili *doll, she is hard plastic with an open crown and glued-on wig. Her eyes are painted similar to those of the number one* Barbie. *In the 21in (53cm) size, mint-in-the-box, she is a real collector's item.*

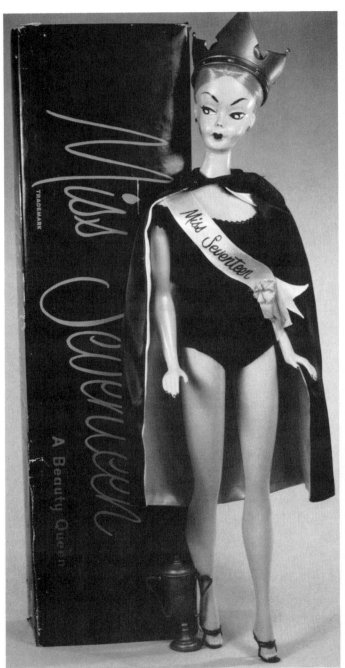

*Illustration 10. Every collector has seen a million of Mattel's Charmin' Chatty® dolls, but this Charmin' Chatty Travels Around the World Gift Set is super hard to find. Here is an example of a common doll that is in an uncommon gift set.*

lecting nostalgia from THEIR past, NOT Europe's past and so are not interested in the outfit. Other collectors, more sophisticated and advanced in their collecting, look at this outfit as elusive and quite valuable.

This is the intrigue with the rare and unusual. Some value it highly while others are not interested at all. To collect this type of item requires a bit of courage, for the burden of proof that the item is genuine rests on you, the seller, should the time come for you to sell it. It is the seller who must produce documentation that the item is indeed rare and not a re-dressed or homemade item.

Before prices went out of sight in the mid 1980s, this question was a mute point. Now, when "prototype" dolls and outfits command upwards of $20,000 for a pre-patented *Barbie* doll and "rare" Madame Alexander dolls can bring $7000 and up, it has fallen upon the seller to provide proof that the item is indeed the real thing.

Doll collectors love to collect dolls. If we all had bottomless checkbooks and lived in mansions, I am sure that antique, collectible, modern and doll artist dolls would fill every nook and cranny and that holidays would bring forth a maze of feather trees, papier-mâché Santas and gilded eggs. However, since limits are placed on 90 percent of us, we must "specialize" in one area of collecting while lusting after ALL the dolls we see advertised in **Doll Reader's®** tempting pages. Yes, it is just these limitations heretofore mentioned that make us turn our backs (and wallets) on the total spectrum of dolldom!

The prudent and educated collector can always spot the rare, the different and the unique in any class of doll. For example, did you know that the Ideal *Toni* doll came in about 50 outfits and that the American Character *Betsy McCall®* had almost as many frocks! Then take into consideration that a simple *Barbie* Pak fashion could come in ten different fabrics and umpteen different combinations of those ten fabrics and you can see why the rare and unusual dolls are those which advanced collectors worship.

Often I am asked in my lectures just what makes an "advanced collector." My definition is someone who has the basics, the easy-to-find, even the hard-to-find, and has made a decision that money is not the motivation behind their collection, for many times they alone can attest to the authenticity of a rare item. The advanced collectors' collections are so much a part of them that it is their heirs and not themselves who will benefit from their zeal, for they would rather die than sell!

As in most fields, knowledge is the key to successful buying whether for fun or for investment, for it is the open mind that is receptive to the possibilities that rare items do exist and the educated mind that can weigh whether the item is genuine and worthy of inclusion in a fine collection.

Often collectors at my many appearances lament the fact that they feel that many dolls are "out of their reach." My reply is "Nonsense," for in my travels, I have seen the rare sell for next to nothing because the seller was not educated, but the collector was.

When **Doll Reader** comes, read ALL the articles, for within those pages is the knowledge of experts. Then you, too, can be like the passer-by in a nearby neighborhood who found a mint *Jumeau* in a trash can, or my lucky friend who found a rare side-part *Barbie* for $1.00 at

***Illustration 11.*** *Everyone loves Ideal's* Tammy *doll, but just recently I was fortunate enough to get this rare-beyond-rare store display featuring the doll and her family.*

a flea market! These finds make us return again and again to the wellspring of knowledge, for to the educated belong the spoils and the victory of an outstanding collection made up of the rare and unusual collectible dolls.

The next time you see something in a dealer's booth that seems different, ASK...for you may learn more than the price of a doll. With education comes power and the ability to collect dolls to the utmost degree with confidence that you are assembling something that will make you and your family proud to display...something unique and RARE! □

Barbie® and *Charmin' Chatty*® are registered trademarks of Mattel, Inc.
*Toni*® is a registered trademark of The Gillette Co.
*Revlon*® is a registered trademark of Revlon, Inc.
*Betsy McCall*® is a registered trademark of the McCall Corp.
*Darci*®, *Dana*® and *Erica*® are registered trademarks of Kenner.

*Illustration 13. We remember Kenner's Darci*® *doll, the gorgeous fashion doll from the late 1970s who resembled the girls seen in the television series, "Charlie's Angels." Few realize that along with her black friend, Dana*®, *there was another friend, Erica*®. *The doll was made late in the production run and her outfits shown in the fashion booklet were never made. She is worth about $100 and up today!*

*Illustration 12. Most celebrity collectors have a World Doll Marilyn Monroe, but this doll is most unique in that instead of wearing the common red dress and white boa, she wears the dress from the movie* The Seven Year Itch. *Allegedly, when World Doll bought the Marilyn rights, they thought all was theirs. It turns out the studio still owned the rights to the dress, so another one had to be designed. Only 900 dolls are wearing this dress!*

# The Many Faces of *Ginny*

*OPPOSITE PAGE: Illustration 1.* The face of Ginny *is truly reflected in this gorgeous strung doll from 1953 and named* Linda.

*RIGHT: Illustration 2.* The first dolls Mrs. Graves dressed were the bisque-headed Just Me *dolls by Armand Marseille. Today, these dolls are very desirable and worth around $1000!*

In 1990, a very important person in the doll world will be honored on the 100th anniversary of her birthdate. This person, while not a household name, did create a doll that was and still is a name everyone recognizes. That name is *Ginny*, and the lady is Jennie Adler Graves, born in Somerville, Massachusetts, May 14, 1890. Before her death in 1971 at age 81, Jennie Graves had done what had not been accomplished before. She holds the honor of creating the longest-lasting American-made doll business, and is credited with making thousands of children and adult collectors happy worldwide!

Mrs. Graves was a woman way ahead of her time. At age 15, her father died, and suddenly the financial picture of the family changed and Jennie had to go to work to help out. Finally, after several menial jobs, Jennie landed a job in a fine lingerie shop in Boston. It was here that her first exposure to quality fabrics took place.

Like most women of her time, marriage and children was really the only choice. Jennie married William H. Graves at the age of 21 and had three children. Not content to sit home and keep house, Mrs. Graves (who had married well), began to sew and donated her projects to charity. It was awhile before she realized that the charity was selling her work for extravagant prices, and Jennie realized there was a market for her skills.

In 1922, she opened the Vogue Doll Shoppe. Always a lover of dolls since childhood, Jennie began buying the German bisque dolls that came in chemises and started dressing them in grand style. Soon it became apparent that the little dolls were the most popular, so Mrs. Graves concentrated on the

*Just Me* dolls made by Armand Marseille. Through clever designing, Jennie soon was turning out trunks, wardrobes and beautiful lingerie for these little dolls. Her "Shoppe" became so popular that it created a traffic jam in the neighborhood and she was forced to relocate elsewhere.

By 1951, she would have two plants in operation, one in Medford and the other in Malden, Massachusetts.

Around the middle of the 1930s, Jennie changed the name to Vogue

Dolls. "Vogue" carried that precious French ambiance of style to it and lended itself to a "couture" definition of her work.

Unfortunately, life sometimes holds many surprises, and around that same period Mrs. Graves husband died and Jennie found herself smack dab in the middle of the Depression with a family, a small business that really had been just for fun, and a dwindling supply of money. Thus Mrs. Graves was forced to compete, in order to make

*Illustration 3. The composition dolls, which took over in the late 1930s, were called Toddles. This World War II soldier reflects several of the patriotic themes available.*

almost every company, started using the new material. Superior in every way to the old composition dolls, hard plastic dolls became the mainstay of the doll business for more than a decade until vinyl replaced many of the harder material models.

Vogue Dolls became a victim of changing tastes as the baby boom children grew up and wanted dolls that represented their idols of the day such as Sandra Dee and others. Children no longer wanted to play in the present, but in the future with dolls that were sophisticated and glamorous.

The other factor was that Mrs. Graves, while on the one hand being very progressive, strongly felt that the selection of a child's toy should be up to the parents and not the youngster. Because of this philosophy, Vogue refused to advertise on television, and soon dolls such as Mattel's *Barbie®*, Ideal's *Revlon®* dolls and a host of others, reached out every afternoon and on Saturday morning with glittering commercials that implied your life was incomplete without owning one of these stunning icons of teenage high fashion.

The new discovery in doll technology was polyvinylchloride or simply "vinyl" as we call it today. This cheaper medium allowed for the mass manufacture of dolls in all sizes and shapes. Some were fantastic and today stand out as outstanding collectibles (such as the *Playpal* series by Ideal that were so lifelike). Others were cheap imitations of the popular dolls of the day like *Barbie®* that cost $1.00 then and are worth about the same today!

By 1965, the Vogue Doll Company was making all-vinyl dolls.

Some were imaginative and clever, some were ghosts of the identity that *Ginny* once had. Later on, by the late 1960s, the dolls were being made from

ends meet, in a man's world which did not welcome her.

Few people realize the impact Mrs. Graves had on American business. In 1952, she single-handedly changed the way small businesses were taxed by appearing in Washington, D.C., before the House Ways and Means Committee.

More importantly, Mrs. Graves was the creator of the doll that made childhood for so many, the *Ginny* doll!

Content for years to use the German *Just Me* dolls, as the condition worsened between Germany and the United States, pre-World War II, it became all too clear that Mrs. Graves would have to develop her own doll. Bernard Lipfert, the famous designer

of the *Shirley Temple* dolls and several other important dolls of the decade, made a toddler doll for Mrs. Graves that she would use for her basic doll from 1937 to 1948.

It was during this period that Virginia Graves Carlson, the daughter of Jennie Graves came to work for the company as the chief designer.

By 1943, the slogan "Fashion Leaders in Doll Society" had been adopted, and the company was doing well. Also a leader in the "cottage industry" area, where workers picked up work and took it home to finish, the Vogue Doll Company was making quite a name for itself.

Finally the golden heyday of plastic arrived and Mrs. Graves, along with

**ABOVE LEFT: Illustration 4.** By 1948, the little dolls were made of all hard plastic and had painted eyes and mohair wigs. The dolls came as little girls and nursery rhyme characters, among others.

**ABOVE RIGHT: Illustration 5.** A "transitional" doll in all hard plastic with sleep eyes in a pale blue dress. She was an Easter special for 1951. Note the pale plastic and muted lip coloring.

**RIGHT: Illustration 6.** This little charmer sports a "Poodle Cut" hairdo, made of caracul (lamb's wool), and was available only in 1952.

the same molds, but in Hong Kong and could no longer compete with the *Alexander-Kins*, made by Madame Alexander, Mrs. Graves' only real rival in the miniature doll category.

In 1970, Jennie Graves retired to Falmouth, Massachusetts, and her daughter Virginia retired to care for her mother.

It is here that the story becomes cloudy for the next few years. Records just do not exist on the sale of the company, rights and so forth, or at least have not been made public.

The next surprise came in 1978 when ads appeared in women's magazines proclaiming "*Ginny*...The doll you loved as a child is back." The problem was the doll did not look a thing like the doll "mother" did love as a child. Neither child or toddler nor attractive, the Lesney *Ginny* dolls never caught on.

Finally in 1984, Walter Reiling, President of Meritus Industries, secured the Vogue doll and *Ginny* rights. This new version of *Ginny* was beautifully done, and had the look of the dolls from the vinyl made in the United

**RIGHT: Illustration 9.** *The late 1950s saw a different coloring to the dolls and bending knees.*

**BELOW: Illustration 10.** *In the early 1960s, cutbacks in quality were showing up. The face is very similar to the face used today.*

States period of the mid 1960s. The quality was high, and the effort was made to make *Ginny* a household word.

The public by this time, however, had basically forgotten the name *Ginny* except as some vague abstract memory from childhood, and it was difficult to connect the name to the product.

Nevertheless, the Meritus dolls were lovely and for almost two years were produced and sold well.

At last, in 1986, the Dakin Company purchased from Wally Reiling the Vogue doll line. By that time, the 1987 line had basically been planned and so Dakin had little input, but by 1988 change was literally bursting at the seams!

The Dakin *Ginny* dolls are beautifully made, and are again bringing joy and happiness to adults and children alike. Made in both hard plastic and vinyl, several price ranges are available to satisfy both the child and the adult collector. In addition, store specials, holiday themes and convention souvenirs are making the Dakin dolls valuable investment dolls as well. It looks

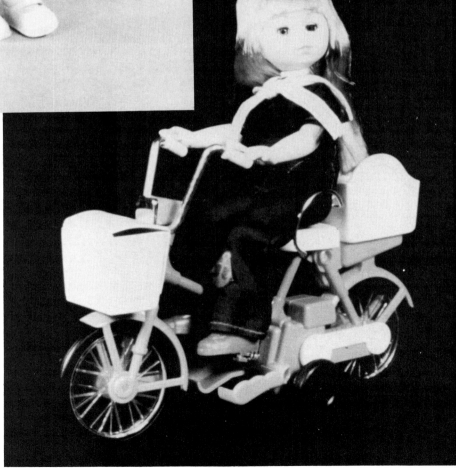

**BELOW: Illustration 12.** The Lesney Company (a division of Matchbox), reissued Ginny in the late 1970s. She did not look anything like her predecessor!

**ABOVE LEFT: Illustration 13.** *Finally, in 1986, Dakin took over the Vogue doll line. This* Miss Ginny *of 1987 is an outstanding collectible.*

**ABOVE RIGHT: Illustration 14.** *In 1988, Dakin issued a* Ginny *in black but was not pleased with the initial batch of 750 dolls. They were recolored with different eyes, making the first issue a collectible.*

**RIGHT: Illustration 15.** *New and imaginative themes are coming from Dakin, such as this* Court Jester!

like *Ginny* has found a wonderful home at last in San Francisco at Dakin headquarters!

Yes, over the years the face of *Ginny* has changed numerous times from little girl to pre-teen and back to little girl. One thing has not changed, however, and that is if Mrs. Graves were alive today to celebrate her 100th birthday, she would surely look at *Ginny* today and love her just as much, and thrill to the joy and happiness that is still apparent today, since the Vogue Doll Shoppe opened that fateful day in 1922! ☐

*Barbie*® is a registered trademark of Mattel, Inc.
*Revlon*® is a registered trademark of Revlon, Inc.

**Illustration 1.** The ultimate fashion doll, the *Revlon* doll, issued in vinyl in 1956. This size is 20in (51cm) and is dressed in "Cherries A La Mode." The dress is made of nylon, a new "miracle" fiber.

# So Beautiful Her Name Just Had to be... *Revlon*

Volumes have been written on the phenomenon of the American teenager. Spawned of a war-weary nation in the mid 1950s, this group developed a culture, a language and a flair all its own. Before then, the "teen" years were ones of transition; a time of movement from the world of the child to the responsible world of adults. From age 13 to 20, a child was expected to gain the maturity, the insight and the education to deal with the demands of the outside world. Realities such as jobs, families and bills required a period of "apprenticeship." These years were ones in which to look up to one's mother or father (or both) and see them as upstanding citizens, worthy of emulation.

All this was the way things were in our nation, for the most part, up until the mid 1950s. Suddenly for the first time ever, the "good life" seemed within most people's grasp. The returning veteran from World War II found a nation reaching out to him with gratitude, offering him tract housing at affordable prices, education made

possible through the GI Bill, and jobs just clamoring for the skills he learned in the service. No longer did survival occupy the minds of our nation. Prosperity and growth were the passwords of the Eisenhower era.

These prosperous parents were having two children (preferably a boy and a girl), but siblings were playing an ever increasing role in the growth of a teenager, especially the American phenomenon of the teenage girl.

By the time a young girl was ready for the magic world of teens, she suddenly found that mother was NOT a good source of information about the world of soda shops, pizza parlors and drive-ins. The mothers of this generation had been forced to skip the fun of living, instead concentrating on coupon rationing, assembly line jobs and survival without their fathers and husbands. What could this type of mother, a woman whose years were spent in worry, possibly be able to tell her daughter about fun? And thus was born ANOTHER American phenomenon, the "big sister."

Lucky indeed was the pre-teen girl who had one, for through her, much information could be gleaned about which mother knew nothing. These teenage girls were LIVING. With skin-tight sweaters and saddle shoes, jitterbugging the night away, these teenage beauties were what the pre-teen dreamed of becoming. Television shows would later focus on them in the form of "The Donna Reed Show," featuring Shelley Fabares as Mary Stone, and "Father Knows Best," starring Elinor Donahue as Betty Anderson. Movies such as *Imitation of Life* would introduce, in 1959, Sandra Dee, THE image that teenage girls strived for. The doll industry, always ready to grab hold of a trend, responded.

As it had once done with Shirley Temple, when her image represented what children wanted to be, The Ideal Toy Corporation, then in Hollis, New York, moved quickly and issued what would soon become the leader of all fashion dolls, the *Revlon* doll.

**Illustration 2.** An Ideal 1953 *Princess Mary*. This doll is on an all hard plastic body marked: "P-93." Her head mold is copied after the *Toni* doll in vinyl and is marked: "V-22." (The author suspects this is the face for the 22in (56cm) *Revlon* doll.)

Collectors define a collectible fashion doll as one having high-heeled feet and a "full figure," a polite way of saying the doll is definitely a woman! In a brilliant marketing strategy, Ideal approached the Revlon Company, headed by Charles Revson, and asked if they could use the name *Revlon*. Ideal had had great success with this concept in the past. Its "name" dolls, such as *Shirley Temple, Deanna Durbin, Judy Garland* and *Mary Hartline*, had been huge commercial hits. So had its use of tie-ins to products that also were identified with glamour. The *Toni* doll, the largest selling doll of the early 1950s, using a license from the Gillette Company, had topped all records. Even the *Harriet Hubbard Ayer* doll, tied to Ayer cosmetics, had been a success. If the *Revlon* doll had a celebrity to be modeled after, it could have really hit the market big.

The dolls first appeared in stores around 1956. One Ideal catalog I have examined from 1955 does not mention

**Illustration 3.** A beautiful 22in (56cm) *Revlon* doll in mint condition. Note the comparison to the *Princess Mary* face, seen in **Illustration 4.** *Edith Willcox Collection.*

Illustration 4. Gorgeous platinum blonde 18in (46cm) *Revlon* doll wearing an extra boxed outfit. Her hairdo is the ponytail style. Also available was a bob style with pulled-back sides.

these dolls, but one brochure in my possession from 1956 includes the very first of these exciting new toys. Had the doll come out three years later, it could have had a celebrity tie-in to the teenage girls who were rapidly becoming household words. Actually the doll was based loosely on a celebrity of sorts, the lovely "Revlon Girl" from the period.

My research for this article took me many place, and I have drawn some conclusions that I feel have enough fact to back them up. Just like a few years ago when a lovely model, Karen Graham, was the uncredited "official" model for Estee Lauder, appearing exclusively without name credit in ALL advertising for these cosmetics, so was young starlet Barbara Britton the spokesperson and model for Revlon in the mid 1950s.

When the dolls appeared in 1956, much was made in the advertising that the doll "looked just like the famous Revlon Girl." Since Barbara Britton WAS the Revlon Girl, but uncredited, I cannot help but feel the *Revlon* dolls were based on not only the "big sister" phenomenon and Revlon cosmetics, but Barbara Britton as well.

Available in 1956 in four sizes, they were made of a high quality vinyl that was heavy, rich and creamy. The 14in (36cm) size (the hardest today to find), the 18in (46cm) and the 20in (51cm) all are marked "VT" (possibly very tall?) and then the size number, and "Ideal Doll." All the dolls had beautiful sleep eyes and thick, wonderfully rooted hair.

In the brochures packed with the dolls, the emphasis on hair play was stressed, stating that "Revlon 'Satin Set' hair spray would keep your doll's hair in place." Seemingly made from new molds, the face did bear a resemblance to Barbara Britton, but also looked vaguely like the hard plastic *Toni* dolls as well.

Another mystery concerning these dolls is that the largest size, 22in (56cm), had a head mold that is, in my opinion, the vinyl face used on Ideal's *Princess Mary* dolls, and the vinyl-headed rare versions of *Toni* and *Mary Hartline*. An examination of a 22in (56cm) *Princess Mary* reveals the exact same mold marks as the Revlon doll, except the "T" on "VT" is not clearly seen. Ideal had great success with the look of the *Toni* doll; it had a proven face.

If this theory is correct, it would have a wonderful sociological conclu-

sion. Little girls had loved playing with dolls that represented themselves as children, such as the *Toni* doll. Now, the FUTURE seemed to a child to hold much promise. Putting that face on an adult body combined a friendly familiar face, but now that face represented the land of teenagers, NOT a toddler.

Madame Alexander challenged the *Revlon* doll with *Cissy*, its entry into the high-heeled fashion doll market. They, too, would take a toddler doll head (*Binnie Walker*) and put it on an adult body. Concentrating on the clothing for which Alexander was famous, and not hair play, *Cissy* would be considered the rich child's fashion doll. Even American Character allowed their toddler doll, *Sweet Sue*, to grow up into *Sweet Sue Sophisticate*, a high-heeled beauty that sported a real bra! Yes, dolls AND children were rapidly growing up into the seemingly glamorous world of teenager.

By 1957, the larger *Revlon* dolls were selling beautifully. The logo on the box stated: "So Beautiful, Her Name Just HAD to be Revlon." Another logo showed a small child overjoyed that she at last had a "big sister" to talk with and share her

**Illustration 5.** A studio publicity shot of Barbara Britton, the "Revlon Girl" of the 1950s. *Movie Star News Photograph.*

secrets. This message emblazed on the box announced: "Little Girls Whisper... NOW I Have a Big Sister." All around the box ran the message: "Beautiful, Beautiful Revlon Doll." Catchy names for outfits such as "Queen of Diamonds," a velvet cocktail dress and white stole with sparkling rhinestone jewelry and the gorgeous "Cherries A La Mode," a party frock in "party pretty DuPont nylon" that featured flocked-on cherry blossoms and a gorgeous straw hat, told the story of future glamour beautifully to a nation of young girls.

That same year, the biggest selling doll of all the *Revlon* dolls was added to the line, *Little Miss Revlon*. A demure 10in (25cm) tall, she was adult perfection, and came in her "Formfit Bra and Girdle." A special message was included to the new little "sister," on the care of the doll. Also included was a fashion booklet that showed how *Little Miss Revlon* could go from art class to square dancing, from nursing to formals, and be glamorous.

**Illustration 6.** Full-length view of the 20in (51cm) *Revlon* doll shown in **Illustration 1.** Her shoes are made of black plastic with elastic straps. On her wrist are two tags, one a fashion booklet and the other stating her dress is of "DuPont Nylon...always party pretty!"

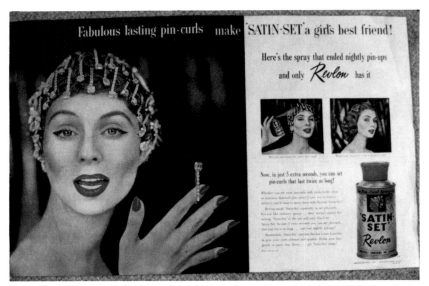

ABOVE: **Illustration 7.** A Revlon ad from the 1950s showing "Satin Set Hair Spray," the official hair spray of the *Revlon* dolls. Cosmetics were a booming industry in the post-World War II era. (Remember all those pin curls?)

RIGHT: **Illustration 8.** Full view of the 22in (56cm) *Revlon* doll seen in **Illustration 3.** The earliest *Revlon* doll boxes did not have the artwork which told the Revlon story. *Edith Willcox Collection.*

**Illustration 9.** Deluxe versions of *Revlon* dolls were availble with fancy ballgowns. This dress is made of blue brocade and black velvet and is labeled. The lid to the box shows the "big sister" concept.

**ABOVE LEFT: Illustration 10.** The rarest *Revlon* dolls were the 14in (36cm) size. This doll wears an original dress, but shoes are replaced. All *Revlon* dolls are marked on their necks: "Ideal Doll."

**ABOVE RIGHT: Illustration 11.** Extra boxed outfits were available for the 18in (46cm) size dolls. The basic dolls in black chemises also came in these striped boxes. Most dolls, however, were sold dressed.

**RIGHT: Illustration 12.** In 1957, the smallest and most popular size appeared, called *Little Miss Revlon*. She was 10in (25cm) of demure sophistication and came wearing her "Formfit Bra and Girdle." The first doll appeared in this diamond block box.

**Illustration 13.** Very hard to find is this *Little Miss Revlon* Gift Set which features the doll and four outfits which varied from set to set. The cardboard box had windows with pop-up awnings on them, as did the extra clothing boxes. It dates from 1957.

**Illustration 14.** Every popular doll is widely imitated. Some even use the same style of writing for logos such as this *Little Miss Renee* by Jolly Toys. The "Renee" is written the same way as "Revlon." The doll is marked: "P (in a circle)." Many *Revlon* imitators have this mark. Dolls must have been sold to many companies, then boxed.

No personality was defined for the dolls; it did not need to be. The fertile imaginations of young girls conjured up many longed-for situations with these dolls. The doll in many ways was the girl herself in a few years (all hair colors were available). The personality was the child's own vision of herself in the future.

Mothers (and fathers) responded differently to this type of doll. Some did not like the doll, and found the full figure offensive and erotic. Other mothers welcomed a "role model" into the child's life to help her make the transition to teenager, something that the mothers did not fully understand. Some parents were worried about their children growing up too fast, and that was a legitimate worry, for "Sweet 16" was THE age to be in the late 1950s. Many women reading this article will fondly remember leaving the house dressed up and made up one way, only to add more make-up and subtract some clothing once out of sight of parents, who were considered "the

**Illustration 15.** The popularity of *Little Miss Revlon* led to later issues in 1958 with beautiful packaging that showed the glamour of her life. Her personality was that of her owner in the future!

enemy"!

By the late 1950s, Ideal head experimented with extra clothing for the larger sizes, but the concept was confusing to the public. Once in the store, one could not remember which size one had, since only 2in (5cm) separated the three largest sizes. Eventually only the 18in (46cm) doll was kept in the line, and extra boxed clothing in the form of cotton dresses and slips were available.

Other innovations appeared on later dolls, such as bending knees and bride dresses, but clearly the arrival of *Barbie®* by Mattel in 1960 had killed off the *Revlon* doll. Even Madame Alexander suffered as sales on *Cissy* declined, as *Barbie* was smartly marketed toward ALL children and available in both the "better" stores and thrift outlets. Also, a brief resurgence in the popularity of life-sized "companion dolls," such as Ideal's own *Patti Playpal*, wiped out the fashion doll market for all but *Barbie*.

The *Revlon* doll had served a purpose. A stepping stone into the adult world, she gave children a preview of life ahead. Collectors of these dolls often view her nostalgically as another "big sister," or perhaps the ONLY sister they had to whisper their secrets and questions to. Like most dolls from the 1950s, the *Revlon* doll is a part of our past we do not want to forget. □

*Barbie®* is a registered trademark of Mattel, Inc.

**Illustration 16.** Fully dressed versions were available in fancy outfits with purses which carried the Revlon name. The *Revlon* doll was the leader of all fashion dolls.

# Twiggy...The MOD Model

The British Invasion of 1964. I remember well where I was when it happened. In English class in my ivy-covered high school, something was being passed around. Finally Barbara Clark, who sat in back of me, thrust something flat in my lap. I picked up the paper-covered object and stared at the photograph of four young men with hair-covered foreheads and strange looking suits. It was a copy of "I Want to Hold Your Hand" by the Beatles. Little did Barbara, the rest of our classmates, or myself know how much that record would change our lives. For the second time in our country's history, we were about to be invaded!

My high school in the mid 1960s was like many suburban buildings. My grandfather was past-president of the school board. My mother had graduated from here. The students, like in many such schools, were mostly college prep. Labels like Brooks Brothers, L.L. Bean and Bobbie Brooks spilled out of shetland sweaters, penny loafers and khaki trousers. To be "daring" meant wearing no socks with one's Bass Weejun loafers!

Of course there were a few post Dion and Fabian types, and there were some girls with "bad" reputations who wore tight sweaters and too much makeup, but they kept to themselves and stole a cigarette in the lavatory between classes. The bulk of the students were more like Wally Cleaver and Mary Stone, and so were our families. All that was about to change forever.

In England, teenagers were rebelling against "the Establishment." Born into a country with more stringent rules, they had more to rebel against. Teens divided themselves into two groups, the "Mods" and the "Rockers." If you were "Mod," you were hip, pretty, often talented and your rebellion was more cosmetic. Dissatisfaction with the status quo was "gently" expressed by perhaps an extreme hair cut, or a short new "mini skirt."

The "Rockers," however, seemed to have more of an axe to grind. They were the real rebels who began to experiment with drugs, and lived an underground type of existence.

In our own country, "rebellion" often meant not doing one's homework

on time, or staying out an extra half hour. The Kennedy influence was still with us as most teenagers here had high aspirations for the future. For most, this generation was often the first one in a family to ever have had the chance to attend college. The future was somewhat secure.

When the Beatles appeared, it is uncanny how so much changed almost overnight. By the end of 1964, the furry moppets would have been on "The Ed Sullivan Show," and had four number one singles. A movie, *A Hard Day's Night*, would unite their fans into "Beatlemania."

All of this had a great effect on the daily lives of American teenagers. I cannot tell you why, but suddenly I did not want to dress like my dad anymore. My family's lovely suburban home often seemed a prison. The status symbols I had worshipped suddenly meant nothing. Fashions began changing so quickly that the next year in school, one could hardly recognize one's friends. The girls now had long, straight hair, and short, short skirts. Even the "good girls" now wore tons of makeup. The boys, never particularly fashion conscious, sported engineer striped or flowered bell bottoms and "Beatle Bang" hair cuts! Like most parents, mine were horrified. The bigger the fuss our families made, the more we rebelled. Oh, I still wanted to go to college, but now I, along with many of my classmates, was MOD! I would not be caught dead in ANYTHING I owned previously. The time was right for part two of the Invasion!

Lesley Hornby was born in 1949 in a working class suburb of London. Always thin as a child, her father had dubbed her "Sticks," because she was skinny as a twig. This led to some of her friends calling her "Twig." When she was 15, she was 5ft 6in tall and weighed 91 pounds. Her measurements were 31-22-32. Not exactly a Marilyn Monroe type, "Sticks" was completely flat-chested and looked more like a boy with long hair. Like many girls from her background, she dated early. One of her dates when she was 15 was a

25-year-old hairdresser, Nigel Davies, who called himself "Justin de Villeneuve" because he thought it sounded more sophisticated. The two became fast friends, and it was he who dubbed her "Twiggy."

Only in the 1960s could a girl built like Twiggy ever have had a chance at success. Rebellion was forcing out the old standards of EVERYTHING, and since no one knew what the "new" standards were, anything could transpire! Once a girl built like Twiggy could have only modeled for posters depicting starving children in some third world country, but in the swinging world of 1960s Mod London, anything could happen! Justin took Twiggy to the well-known Mr. Leonard, super hairdresser (or "crimper") who lightened her hair, and cut it into her signature hair style, a boyish short cut with long bangs which draped across her forehead and wrapped behind her ear.

In just one short year, Justin de Villeneuve would become Svengali to Twiggy. Acting as boyfriend, bodyguard, mentor and merchandiser, he knew Twiggy was catching on fast. Mr. Leonard believed that his hair style was an exciting new one. He ran a photograph of Twiggy in a London newspaper with the caption: "This is the face of 1966." It soon became apparent that both the hair style AND the face were being noticed. Within months, Twiggy was the top model in London and Paris. A cover on the magazine *Elle* made Justin realize there was another world to conquer — America!

Twiggy arrived in the United States on March 20, 1967, creating a media blitz not seen since the arrival of the Beatles three years earlier. Twiggy was received by President Johnson, was a guest of Disneyland, and unveiled her new dresses and other Twiggy merchandise. Yardley of London, long a conservative cosmetic company for blue-haired dowager ladies, launched an exciting line of makeup and false eyelashes, capitalizing on the London connection. Soon teenage girls were participating in Twiggy look-alike

**OPPOSITE PAGE: Illustration 1.** *Twiggy*®, the Mod Model of the late 1960s, interpreted in doll form by Mattel in 1967. This doll is all vinyl with rooted eyelashes and hair.

**Illustration 2.** *Twiggy*® could wear all of *Francie's*® MOD fashions. These outfits really are period pieces. The go-go boots, miniskirts and patterned tights are all 1960s chic. The background polka dot wallpaper was on the author's bedroom walls in 1967!

**Illustration 3.** *Twiggy*® models "*Twiggy*® Turnouts," one of four extra outfits available for the doll.

**Illustration 4.** A rare black version of *Francie*® models with friends *Casey*®, *Twiggy*® and *Francie*®. A piece of history is captured in these dolls and their fashions.

contests. Licensed products such as notebooks, jewelry boxes, T-shirts, board games and bubble gum cards pushed her earnings beyond $3,000,000!

By now I was in college. My grades were sufficient, but there was always time to shop the trendy boutiques of New York and Philadelphia. Like most teens, I spent every dime I earned at part-time jobs on records or clothes! Resigned to my fate of having to attend school, I was at least going to look like I did not. All this change was not unnoticed by the toy industry.

At Mattel, creators of *Barbie*, there was much flurry of activity. *Barbie* had been created in the late 1950s. This now seemed like a lifetime ago. Today's child was completely different from the child of just ten short years ago. Mattel was earning millions off the sale of *Barbie*. Her personality was that of her young owner, and her wardrobe reflected that. In 1959 little girls wanted to be a nurse, a ballerina or a bride. What on earth did they want now! The reader of the personal part of this article may conclude that I was somewhat spoiled. Like many teenagers of the time, I had been sheltered from the realities of the world. Many of us saw life through a television screen that looked like June Cleaver's living room. For us, poverty, crime, wars and assassinations were like a distant cloud, something that "others" experienced.

In my interview with Ruth Handler, creator of *Barbie*, in February 1986, we discussed this topic at length. (Ruth and Elliot Handler were the recipients of the 1986 DOTY® Lifetime Achievement Award.) Ruth was very concerned what role *Barbie* should project in 1967. The baby boom children were discovering that life was not all the bed of roses they thought it was. No longer could one turn away from Vietnam, drugs, poverty and all the social ills that beset America. Minorities were demanding their rights as well. It was the most confusing time in our country's history.

Ruth felt that *Barbie* could go MOD, but never change her basic personality. Causes, demonstrations and other activities were not something *Barbie* would participate in. As a sheltered teenager from Willows High (a fictitious high school in Wisconsin), her life was much like mine and that of millions of others. Her "rebellion" as it were, would only be expressed through CLOTHING. Ruth commented that during the late 1960s, the personality

of *Barbie* was made more nondescript. *Barbie* simply AVOIDED. Soon critics would change that word to APATHY, but it would not matter.

Mattel did feel that the Mod influence was too strong to be ignored, and so played up the FUN aspects of the time period by securing the rights to a *Twiggy* doll! The doll, made from the *Casey* head mold, and having the *Francie* body, was perfect. Packaged in a see-through carton, the box had a gorgeous full color pin up of Twiggy to display on your mirror. Available also were four outfits with names such as "Twiggy Gear," (gear meaning clothing) and "*Twiggy* Turnouts" (turnedout meaning all dressed up in Mod slang). Other outfits were "*Twiggy*-Do's" and "Twigster." All were miniskirt designs, very short and very MOD. The doll was an instant success and led Mattel to put its name on Twiggy

LEFT: **Illustration 5.** Never opened mint-in-the-box *Twiggy* doll. This celebrity doll was *Barbie's* MODern cousin, *Francie's* friend. The doll came with a cutout poster of Twiggy. **BELOW: Illustration 6.** The author, A. Glenn Mandeville, in 1967. Note the Twiggy type hair cut, which was popular with both girls and boys. The suit is "Edwardian," also MOD, but with a Brooks Brothers tie!

**Illustration 7.** All four extra outfits shown with all original accessories. They are from left to right: "*Twiggy®* Gear," "*Twiggy®* Turnouts," "Twigster" and "*Twiggy®*-Do's." *Sara Sink Eames Collection. Photograph by Bob Eames.*

**Illustration 8.** The clothing boxes for the *Twiggy®* outfits ha fabulous artwork depicting a London Mod Model!

**Illustration 9.** Lesley Hornby, better known as "Twiggy," in a publicity still from 1967. *Movie Star News photograph.*

notebooks, jewelry boxes and other merchandise that showed the skinny young model at work and play. Made of vinyl, the 10in (25cm) doll had "rooted eyelashes" and rooted hair.

Ruth Handler told me that this well-timed doll, along with *Barbie®'s MODern Cousin Francie®*, enabled them to ease *Barbie®* through the turbulent late 1960s! *Twiggy®* and *Francie®* and her friend *Casey®* became the embodiment of young London Mod, but could be discontinued if the fad died a quick death. *Barbie®*, just skimming the surface of the Mod movement, would make it through intact. By the early 1970s, it would all be over.

As for Twiggy, she retired from modeling in 1969 and married an actor, Michael Whitney. Their daughter, Carly, was born in 1979. They separated shortly after and Twiggy decided to revitalize her career and become an actress. Her first movie, full of camp humor, was Ken Russell's 1971 musical *The Boy Friend*. It was very well received. She frequently was seen dur-

ing the 1970s in many television and stage performances. In 1981, she made it to Broadway with Tommy Tune in "My One and Only." Twiggy had come a long, long way. No longer the cockney little girl, today Twiggy is a woman of the 1980s, ever growing in both her personal and professional life.

In my own life, well, I decided that maybe my parents were not so terrible after all. Today I wear many of the Shetland sweaters my mother fortunately saved until, as she said, "You came to your senses." I realize the world is not all fun for everybody, and support many personal causes. Being involved in the doll world makes me still a little crazy, but what a way to go!

I would not trade my memories of my flowered bell bottoms for all the button-down shirts in the world! Yes, today I again wear Brooks Brothers suits, but my heart, like Twiggy's, is still MOD! □

**Credits:**
*Twiggy*, by Twiggy. Hawthorn Books, Inc., New York, 1968.

*Twiggy* paper doll set, Whitman, authorized by Minnow Co. Ltd., 1967.
*Total Television*, Alex McNeil. Penguin Books, 1984.
*The Pop Sixties*, Andrew J. Edelstein. World Almanac Publications, 1985.
*Twiggy, Queen of Mod.* Board game by Milton Bradley, 1967, authorized by Minnow Co. Ltd., 1967.
*Twiggy* Notebook by Mattel and Twiggy Enterprises Ltd, 1967.
Author's portrait, Eastern Galleries, Philadelphia, Pennsylvania, 1967.
*Movie Star News,* New York, New York, publicity photographs.

The author would like to thank Sara Sink Eames for the photograph of the complete set of *Twiggy* outfits and her husband, Bob, for taking the photograph. Also, after writing this, I see my parents, Melissa Middleton Mandeville and Arthur J. Mandeville, as being more understanding than I ever gave them credit for!

---

**BELOW LEFT: Illustration 10.** The life of Twiggy was told in this autobiography published by Hawthorn Books, Inc., in 1968. It showed a cockney girl's rise to unexpected fame and her exploitation. **CENTER: Illustration 11.** Original catalog page from a Mattel fashion booklet in 1967 showing the entire *Twiggy®* line. **BELOW RIGHT: Illustration 12.** Fabulous paper doll sets of Twiggy such as this one by Whitman in connection with Minnow Co. Ltd. appeared in 1967. Included was a paper dress for the child! Paper dresses were included in Twiggy's line of clothing.

**BELOW LEFT: Illustration 13.** Mattel also had licensed products, such as this notebook, which the author used in school! **CENTER: Illustration 14.** The Twiggy phenomenon even included a board game by Milton Bardley where you could be "Queen of Mod." **BELOW RIGHT: Illustration 15.** A Ken Russell musical featured Twiggy in 1971. Most people thought Twiggy was just a fad, but she proved otherwise in this successful movie. Shown here is the sound track album where she showed she could sing, too!

Illustration 16. In the 1980s, Twiggy teamed up with Tommy Tune on Broadway for "My One and Only," as seen here in this publicity shot. *Movie Star News Photograph.*

# Ideal Dolls...The End of an Era

**Illustration 1.** One of the first *Patti Playpal* dolls, this 36in (91cm) version is mint-in-box and a non-walker. The hair style is much different. She is made of rigid vinyl with rooted hair and sleep eyes and is marked "Ideal Doll, G35." *Colleen Giles Collection.*

At the 1986 Toy Fair in New York City, New York, buyers who had made their annual mid winter pilgrimage to see what is new in the world of dolls, received a surprise. One of the oldest and most famous of all doll manufacturers had closed their doors to the toy buying public. Ideal was another victim of constantly changing public taste and management techniques. This longtime firm, best remembered for making *Shirley Temple* dolls for three different generations, would not be showing a 1986 line. My opinion is that Ideal was caught in the dice game between quality versus price, independent specialty store versus giant toy supermarkets. Trying to please everyone, they wound up pleasing no one. The quality of Ideal dolls slipped and the public found the name "Ideal" was not enough to carry new lines introduced in the 1980s. Other toy companies who today seem to be resting on past reputations should take heed of this valuable lesson. Also, as in any business, internal problems took their toll. However, we as collectors and aficionados of beauty, can look back at Ideal with an eye that is satisfied. This firm produced an entire genre of dolls that will be forever remembered in the early 1960s, "The Companion Doll."

To begin our story, it is necessary to look at society as a whole in the 1950s. A depression and war weary nation was tired of "making do." Women, now mothers of children born of husbands whom many thought they would never see again after World War II, had grown up during a frugal time. Cheated out of many a chance to have materialism play a part in their lives, they wanted their children to have the storybook life they were denied. The generation of children born after World War II, called "baby boomers," were to be denied nothing. A whole new way of raising children developed as the motives for having children changed. No longer were several siblings needed as extra field hands or house managers. The new generation of post World War II parents were having fewer children out of CHOICE, and treating them to a "Disneyesque" lifestyle. By the late 1950s these children were around 10 years old and ready to have

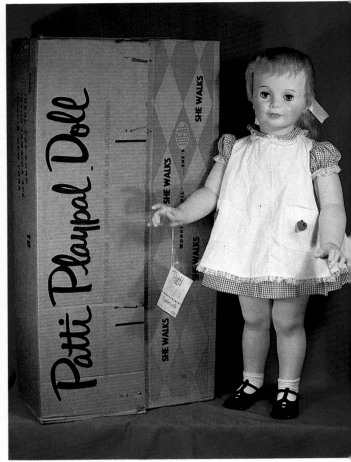

**Illustration 2.** A later *Patti Playpal*, this one is a walker and the box states this fact. Long silky hair is now a trademark of this doll. The wrist tag applauds the fact she can wear real children's clothing. She is marked "Ideal Doll, G35." *Colleen Giles Collection.*

**Illustration 3.** A very rare carrot red-haired *Patti Playpal*, conside by collectors to be the most desirable hair color. *Gidget Donne Collection.*

bestowed on them the opulence and luxury that no generation before had the chance to receive.

Toy companies responded to that need with lavish, gorgeous high-priced dolls. This period is often referred to as "The Golden Age" in collectible dolls, because so many beautiful hard plastic and vinyl dolls were being manufactured. Madame Alexander seemed to lead the line with expensive unbelievable creations made for the wealthy or those who wished they were. Hardly a household with a little girl did not have a bedroom wherein dwelled the little princess and her dolls. The 1950s child on the whole had had beautiful and lovely dolls since birth. Time was ripe for a new idea.

Ideal, a forerunner in the 1930s and 1940s with its celebrity dolls such as *Shirley Temple* and *Deanna Durbin*, found a new idea: A life-size walking doll that a child could take with her, a sort of friend, undeniably an equal in size and beauty to the child itself. These dolls, made of a heavy rigid vinyl, were first strung, then a walking

mechanism added the realistic dimension of the child taking the doll for a stroll. Added to this was another feature. Doll clothes were no longer a problem, as the doll was a child's size three, and could "share" all her clothes. Clever mothers who could sew, could create entire matching outifts for child and doll; even "twins" were a creative possibility.

In my opinion, these dolls served even another purpose. They took the place of other siblings, relieving parents of some of the "guilt" of not having more children. Now a family, choosing to have a boy and a girl, could have that girl "own" her own "little sister," as it were. The mother and father, raised in larger families as was the custom of the 1930s, were somewhat worried what being an "only child" would do for children. Even two-child families were in untested waters. Doctor Spock was having a free hand in telling these mothers what was best as to not "scar" the delicate egos of the baby boomers. In some ways, these companion dolls helped children

through that period when mommy and daddy were not enough. Now they had their own life-size friend. In an era before television and other distractions had fully taken over children, this "friend" must have served a great purpose in the life of a little girl.

Interestingly, Ideal made a boy walking doll as a mate to its *Patti Playpal* series, and named him *Peter*. Company advertising was careful to not come right out and say he was for little boys, but it was implied. Some forward thinking people have always realized that the needs of little boys and little girls are not as far apart as one would think. Boys, too, needed that imaginary friend to tell their secrets to, to laugh with and cry on. It is only today that psychologists are applauding boys having dolls as friends, and view it as a healthy sign to see a little boy and his *Cabbage Patch Kid™*. Perhaps the executives at Ideal in the early 1960s saw a potential market in their *Peter Playpal* as a boy's toy.

Whatever the reason these dolls were bought for, they were a fresh,

**Illustration 4.** 38in (97cm) mint-in-box *Peter Playpal*, all original. His wrist tag states he can wear a real little boy's clothes. He is marked "Ideal, B35-38." *Colleen Giles Collection.*

**Illustration 5.** 32in (81cm) *Penny*, smaller sister to *Peter Playpal* and *Patti Playpal*, mint-in-box and perfect. Her facial sculpting is superb. She is wearing her original organdy clothes and is marked "Ideal Doll, 32-EL." *Colleen Giles Collection.*

innovative idea whose timing was right for so many reasons. Ideal was even creative enough to make a 36in (91cm) version of *Shirley Temple*, and call it *Shirley Temple Playpal*.

Special indeed, this doll had play possibilities that were endless. Mothers had grown up with *Shirley Temple*, and now on television reruns were making this generation love "America's Sweetheart" as much as those who had gone before. Ideal even sold the heads to this doll separately so that *Patti Playpal* could be turned into a *Shirley* doll with a simple home adjustment.

Soon Ideal, knowing a winner, released other dolls in the *Playpal* family. An even larger doll, *Daddy's Girl*, a full 42in (109cm), provided the older child (or the strong young child!) with an almost eerie life-size companion. Younger versions of the family, *Suzy* and *Penny*, and even the *Saucy Walker* size doll became the rage. Bedrooms looked like department stores, as children and their mannequins slept together, dressed together and played together.

**Illustration 6.** 42in (107cm) *Daddy's Girl* is the largest of the companion dolls. She is all original and is marked on the back of her head "Ideal Doll Corp." She is a difficult doll to find today. *Colleen Giles Collection.*

Other companies, realizing they were missing the boat, so to speak, jumped in. Madame Alexander made *Joanie* and *Betty*, Effanbee had *Mary Jane*, Vogue made a 36in (91cm) *Ginny* carrying a standard 8in (20cm) *Ginny* that was on the market a short while, and several "generic" brand walking dolls were available at every source from the supermarket to the hardware store. The early 1960s catalogs from Sears, Roebuck and Co.; J.C. Penneys and Montgomery Ward show these dolls in great abundance until around 1965, when changing tastes, and a doll named *Barbie*, would relegate these dolls to part of our collecting history.

To those who understand them and love them, this type of quality will not be seen again. Dolls so beautiful, so lifelike and so well made do not come along that often. The "companion" doll is one which has a great place of honor in our collectors' world! □

*Cabbage Patch Kid* is a registered trademark of Original Appalachian Artworks, Inc.
*Barbie* is a registered trademark of Mattel Toys, Inc.

◊

**Illustration 7.** 28in (71cm) and 32in (81cm) *Saucy Walkers*, smaller sisters in the *Playpal* family. The doll on the left is marked "Ideal Toy Corp T28x-60" and the one on the right is marked "Ideal Toy Corp, BYE 32-35." *Colleen Giles Collection.*

**FAR RIGHT: Illustration 8.** 36in (91cm) *Shirley Temple Playpal.* Ideal combined two great ideas in the use of a celebrity doll head and name on a popular sized doll. These dolls came dressed in the *Patti* dresses and also in some *Shirley Temple* movie costumes such as those from "Heidi" and "Captain January." She is marked "Ideal Doll, ST 35-38-2." Some dolls have jointed wrists and some do not. *Colleen Giles Collection.*

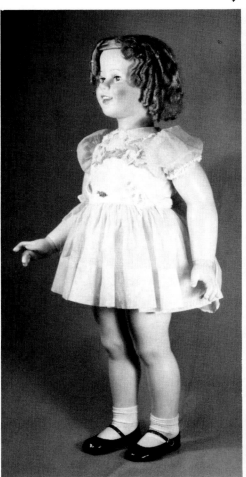

**Illustration 9.** 30in (76cm) *Lori Martin* as *National Velvet*. This doll capitalized on the companion doll fame and was available in several sizes. Her shirt is replaced. The facial modeling is wonderful and makes her a desirable doll.

**RIGHT: Illustration 10.** 16in (41cm) versions of *Patti Playpal* by Ideal. Some of these were walkers and some were strung dolls, but all had the "look" of their big sister. Advertising referred to them as *Petite Patti* and *Tiny Patti*. They are marked "Ideal Toy Corp G18." *Colleen Giles Collection.*

**BELOW: Illustration 11.** Ideal made many variations in the hair styles for *Patti*. This less common style has no bangs, but just little spit curls around the forehead. She is a lovely version of this popular companion doll. *Gidget Donnelly Collection.*

**BELOW RIGHT: Illustration 12.** This all original brunette *Patti* is a desirable collector's doll today as brunettes were, and still are, less common than other colors. Reportedly, one brunette doll left the factory for every 100 blondes! *Gidget Donnelly Collection.*

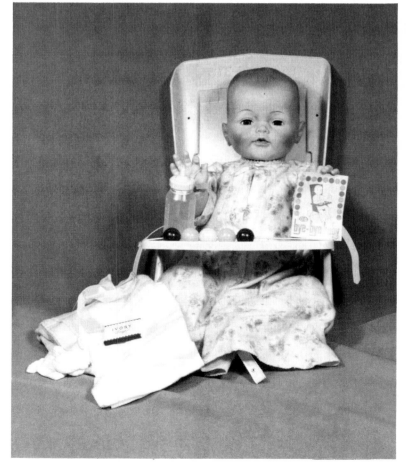

**Illustration 13.** 32in (81cm) *Miss Ideal*. Here Ideal in 1961 was trying to combine the fashion doll craze started by their own *Little Miss Revlon* with the companion doll fad. The feature on this doll was that she was a photographer's model. Already the threat of *Barbie®* was making manufacturers respond. *Colleen Giles Collection.*

**Illustration 14.** 25in (64cm) version of *Miss Ideal*. The booklet tells of the endless hair styling possibilities that this doll has. Ideal was again desperately trying to hold onto the competitive edge over smaller fashion dolls, but by 1965 large dolls would all but vanish.

**Illustration 15.** Rare 25in (64cm) *Bye Bye Baby* with car seat. Life-size baby dolls were a natural extension of the *Playpal* series. This doll is modeled unbelievably lifelike. She is marked "Ideal Toy Corp 5NB." *Colleen Giles Collection.*

# The World of Alexander-Kins

**LEFT: Illustration 1.** The year 1953 saw the introduction of *Wendy-Ann*, a charming all hard plastic 8in (20cm) doll. Made of high quality plastic, she came dressed in lush fabrics. Her wig, made of saran, was washable, and her eyes opened and closed! She represented the "baby boomers" beautifully! **RIGHT: Illustration 2.** This little doll was a "reject," sold to me by a former Alexander employee. I cannot find any flaw on her at all! Because of this, she did not get a wig, but looks adorable anyway!

The year 1953 was important for the Madame Alexander Company. Two major new releases enhanced the already prestigious reputation of this firm. The first was the *Coronation Group* of dolls depicting the recent Coronation of Queen Elizabeth II. A scene was made showing the Queen, with her six attendants, leaving Westminster Abbey, along with ladies-in-waiting. Utilizing her standard dolls, but with different facial painting, Madame Alexander donated this outstanding exhibit to the Brooklyn Children's Museum.

The second event was the release of *Wendy-Ann*, a doll named for Madame Alexander's granddaughter, in a new medium, hard plastic, and a new size, 8in (20cm). Affectionately called *Alexander-Kins*, (kin being a suffix for miniature), these outstanding dolls were an instant hit, and started a new line of creations that today is still the mainstay of Alexander dolls!

Hard plastic was an exciting new material for dolls. Madame Alexander had used a standard 7in (18cm) composition doll for many years and dressed it as dozens of different characters.

Because of its demure size, the fragility of the composition seemed all the more so. Composition was difficult to mold into miniature, as facial details requiring sculpting, such as ears and noses, tended to "flatten out" when pulled from the molds. Also, trapped air caused bubbles around the noses to affect the dolls. Clearly a new design was needed, and artists at the company came up with a beautiful lifelike face and body, made entirely of the new plastic material.

As I have stated many times, Madame Alexander was a clothing designer in doll form. By this time, she had proved this by winning the Fashion Academy Award for clothing design three years in a row. It should also be noted that this award was not just for doll clothing, but for ALL clothing. A list of her competitors would read like a who's who in the garment industry. Madame Alexander concerned herself mainly with the design of new outfits and wigs to make her standard dolls into hundreds of different characters. She never has nor ever will consider herself a doll artist. Her dolls are merely mannequins upon which she displayed her talents with fabrics, a talent that today, even in her 90s, still serves her well.

With just a few alterations over the years, the little face on the *Alexander-Kins* has been the mannequin for literally hundreds of storybook, nursery rhyme and historical characters.

Actually, it was quite a job to pick slides for this article, as almost a THOUSAND different characters came to life on *Wendy-Ann's* little face, and all were stunning. Any selected would have been "the best," for ALL are worthy of collecting!

The real start of the *Alexander-Kins* line in 1953 came at Toy Fair in

**Illustration 3.** A very rare 1953 *Quiz-Kin Bride* and *Groom.* Both have buttons on their backs which make their heads nod yes or no. The *Groom* has a caracul wig made of lambskin!

New York, when 32 different characters created from one mold were introduced! These diverse creations included *Peter Pan*, a *Little Southern Girl*, *Victoria*, *Little Madaline*, and assorted toddlers dressed in frilly children's outfits.

The choice of fabrics was outstanding. Real organdies and cottons, the finest in straw hats and ribbons, all went into the clothing on these dolls. The detailing was so exact that one examining these garments today wishes that our own clothing could be so well made. Madame Alexander always insured that her doll clothing was perfect enough to be worn (if enlarged) by the grandest ladies, gentlemen and children!

That year a show called "The Quiz Kids" was on national television. On the show, precocious tots answered questions for prizes. Madame developed her 8in (20cm) doll to have a new feature, two buttons on the back which allowed the doll to say "yes" or "no," depending on which button was pushed!

It should be noted that the Vogue Doll Company was having quite a success with *Ginny*, who by this time was well established as a play staple. (For more information on *Ginny*, see *Ginny...An American Toddler Doll* by A. Glenn Mandeville, Hobby House Press, Inc.) It has always been traditional in this country for manufacturers to "borrow" ideas from one another, expand them and try to top the competition. This was fairly easy in Madame Alexander's case, as her reputation for

**Illustration 4.** The year 1954 saw the addition of a walker mechanism to the dolls. This great doll is *Mary Louise*, the "shadow" size doll to a larger doll offered that year. Her stock number is 0035D.

**Illustration 5.** *Wendy-Ann* walker from 1954 dressed for the Easter Parade.

pride of the line. With names such as *Apple Annie, Cheri, Agatha* and *Mary Louise* (some of which were "shadows" or smaller versions of larger dolls), publicity for these dolls was in full swing.

By 1955, the charming story *Little Women* had also been utilized for *Alexander-Kins.* They proved so popular that they have been a part of the line in some form, from then up to the present. Because Vogue was doing so well with storybook characters, the line this year included Madame's interpretations of such fables as *Curly-locks, Hansel and Gretel, Romeo and Juliet* (with a rare license to use the actual costumes) and many many others. Most collectors consider 1955 and 1956 to be the "golden" years for these little dolls.

The year 1956 saw the introduction of bending knees to the *Alexander-Kins* line. This company, as well as others such as Strombecker, was making furniture for miniature dolls. The bending feature allowed the little dolls to sit realistically at miniature tables and chairs. The year 1956 also saw Madame rekindle her interest in *Gone with the Wind,* as not only *Scarlett* was available, but *Melanie* and a *Southern Belle* as well. Even a nurse doll was issued! The dolls were so popular that extra boxed clothing was sold for them. Highly priced, they were available only in "better" stores, and included riding habits, ice and roller skating costumes, sleepwear and school dresses. Made in very limited quantities, they are difficult to find today. The gulf was widening between *Ginny* and *Alexander-Kins!*

Play habits of children were beginning to change in the late 1950s. Eager to grow up into a world free of depressions and wars, the early "baby boomers" wanted to get on with life. Movies that focused on teenagers were becoming popular. Little girls, once not eager to grow up into little more than servants, were hearing the call of a glamorous life, made accessible to them through new technologies, that before was available to only a privileged few such as movie stars or models.

The toy companies, Madame Alexander included, responded to this need, especially in the wealthy, by issuing *Cissy* and *Cissette,* their entry into the high-heeled fashion doll market. In 1957, perfect little *Cissette,* a 10in (25cm) wonder of sophistication, made her debut. Afraid of losing the very

catering to the wealthier child, allowed *Wendy-Ann* to arrive with a built-in status. *Ginny,* being sold in some outlets that Alexander would never associate with, was basically a middle-class play doll. *Wendy-Ann* and *Alexander-Kins,* bearing the status of the Alexander name and the aura of stores such as Lord & Taylor, B. Altman's and F.A.O. Schwarz, seemed to be aimed at upper-class children, who tended to treat their dolls as a collection, displayed on shelves, rather than a play situation on the living room floor. Added to this was the fact many Depression mothers, denied dolls by a quirk of events, were eager to set up their daughters in grand style as the princess of the family.

Girls from the period tend to remember having both dolls, *Ginny* being more of a "companion" to their daily lives, while the *Alexander-Kins* seemed more of a "shelf doll". (Ironically, today it is harder to find a mint *Ginny,* because of her play image.) Interestingly, the differences between the two dolls seems to be one of image as the cost between the two for most models was minimal.

In 1953, these dolls were strung with a rubber band, and consisted of a basic five-piece construction. The year 1954 saw the faces remain basically the same, but a "walker" mechanism was added to give more realism to the dolls. The little girls were popular, but a higher-priced character doll was the

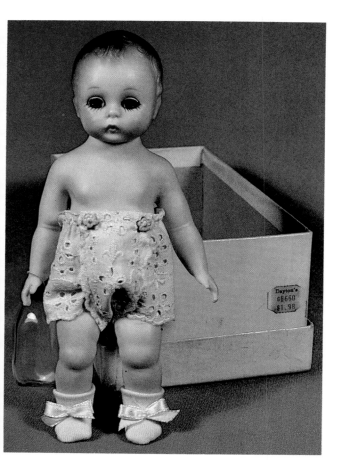

**ABOVE LEFT: Illustration 6.** Madame Alexander wanted children to learn about the past. This little *Godey Lady* from 1955, number 491, taught little girls about fashions of a time long past. **ABOVE RIGHT: Illustration 7.** The tie-in to Walt Disney was irresistible to Madame Alexander. This *Cinderella* from 1955, number 492, is based on the costume from the fairy tale. The Alexander company avoided royalties by basing the dolls on literature rather than films. **BELOW RIGHT: Illustration 8.** Separate furniture was sold for *Wendy*. Made of fabric-covered wood with metal legs, it had a gold sticker identifying it as "Alexander." The rug is also from the living room set. This furniture is still being used in the showroom in New York today! **BELOW LEFT: Illustration 9.** Some interesting combinations of materials appeared in the 1950s. This little doll has a hard plastic head on a toddler one-piece stuffed vinyl body. His box is from Dayton's, a store in the Midwest.

**LEFT: Illustration 10.** The trademark of Madame Alexander was the use of imaginative fabrics and brilliant designs. This little girl is *Wendy calls on a School Friend* and is from 1956, stock number 594. **RIGHT: Illustration 11.** Madame Alexander was said to be so fascinated with *Gone With The Wind* that she locked herself in her room for three days to read it! This little *Scarlett* is one of hundreds of *Scarlett O'Hara* dolls made over the years. She is from 1956.

lucrative market in *Alexander-Kins*, the company tried to tie them together with matching furniture such as brass beds and even matching wardrobes in 1958. Trying to "ease" the transition from child to teen, the company was trying to shake the "baby" image of *Alexander-Kins*.

Retailers also were fearful of losing a large segment of their business, and so billed the little dolls as "collectors items," so that a young girl would not stop "collecting," as it were, these lovely dolls. (Much of this spelled trouble for *Ginny* at this point, because Vogue had ironically tried to stress the "play" value of *Ginny*.)

In 1959, the emphasis was again on making *Wendy* grow up. (The name *Wendy-Ann* had been changed in 1954 due to the unfortunate death of Madame's granddaughter.) Neither the boxes, clothing labels nor wrist tags had *Wendy* on them after 1954. Only the brochures packed in each doll box gave a name to an outfit, such as "Wendy does the Mambo." Bridal fashions and long dresses were put on the little *Alexander-Kins* in an attempt to make the little dolls "grow up."

By 1960, the focus softened somewhat as the high fashion doll lost some appeal. Big dolls, such as Madame's 36in (91cm) *Joanie* and 30in (76cm) *Betty*, were all the rage. It was "safe" to let the *Alexander-Kins* go back to being little girls in frilly outfits again as they had a seemingly secure future as "shelf dolls."

Madame Alexander during this period had created specials for F.A.O. Schwarz over the years with the little dolls, and in 1961 issued *Wendy* in a wicker sewing basket with outfits ready to sew! Manufacturers were desperately trying to keep little girls little. It was a losing battle, however, and final defeat came with the introduction of *Barbie®*, who by late 1960 was rapidly becoming an American icon.

In 1961, the first "Internationals" using *Alexander-Kins* were issued. Advertised as promoting goodwill among foreign nations, the real motivation was probably to keep the little dolls a series collectible. Soon children and young girls together could share a tour of the world through *Alexander-Kins*, and collectibility could continue all through high school for many girls.

It was a brilliant marketing strategy.

As the early 1960s progressed, the company issued some dolls called *Wendy-Kins*, in an attempt to keep the little girl image. (All the dolls were still bending-knee walkers.) *Wendy-kins* had the lovely clothing and accessories that had made Madame famous, but it was the ever-growing International Collection that was the staple of the little doll line.

The last little girl *Wendy-Kins* appeared in 1965. The day of the child playing with an image of herself had vanished. Today's child played in the future, and both *Ginny* and *Wendy* were victims of changing social mores and play patterns. This author had examined some authentic non-walker *Wendy-Kins* made late in 1965, when the walker mechanism was dropped from the little dolls.

From 1966 to the present, storybook, literature and international characters have carried the line, and quite beautifully. The year 1987 has seen the reintroduction of the "Maggie" face (a watermelon grin) on some of the dolls.

While we certainly have beautiful dolls today from the Alexander

Company, we cannot help but miss *Wendy-Ann*, and the view of upper-class life she gave us. Today, perfect examples of these dolls are much sought after, and well they should be, for *Wendy* tells so much of a gracious time in our lives. □

Note: Those of you attending the United Federation of Doll Clubs, Inc., 38th Annual Convention in Boston, August 10 to 14, can see this article expanded greatly in a slide presentation by Mr. Mandeville, made possible by a grant from Hobby House Press, Inc.

The author would like to thank Ann Tardie for her help as a consultant on this project.

*Barbie*® is a registered trademark of Mattel, Inc.

**TOP LEFT: Illustration 12.** One of the things that make Alexander dolls so collectible is that, unlike today, the company showed a new line almost every year. This *Southern Belle*, from 1963, number 385, is from one year only. Economics make this unfeasible today. **ABOVE RIGHT: Illustration 13.** The last year for *Wendy-Kins* was 1965. This little doll lacks the frills that 1950s children had. Times were changing! Her stock number is 662. **LEFT: Illustration 14.** In 1968, at the request of Frank Martin, the West Coast sales representative for Madame Alexander, 300 pieces of a special *Easter Doll* were made. In a letter, Mr. Martin stressed the future value of these dolls. He certainly was correct as today's value is well over $1000! **CENTER LEFT: Illustration 15.** A very rare sample of a *Tinker Bell* doll made for Disney World in the 1970s, but not marketed. The doll is authentic, as a publicity photograph of Madame Alexander's personal collection showed this doll prominently displayed behind her!

# 35 years with *Betsy McCall*

**Illustration 1.** 14in (36cm) *Betsy McCall* doll, 1952 by Ideal. The doll has a hard plastic body, legs and arms (same as the *Toni* doll), with a soft vinyl head with sleep eyes and glued-on saran pageboy wig. Her dress was one of three styles available.

It is difficult today to find someone who does not recognize the name "Betsy McCall." For 35 years, this little girl with the watermelon grin has been friend and fashion model to several generations of children who loved and adored her. Unlike other fashion dolls, such as *Barbie®, Betsy McCall* was a child, doing little girl things and living an upper middle class life long before "Yuppie" became popular. To "young" mothers, she has been a friend and confidant, and to "big" mothers, a source of play value in both paper and solid doll form.

*Betsy McCall* was officially born in print May 1951 in the highly successful *McCall's* magazine, long a staple in the American home. Betsy was not the first of the McCall siblings, but certainly the most famous and long lasting. Her ancestors, like the magazine, were named for a Scotsman, James McCall. In 1925, the well established woman's monthly published a paper doll entitled, "Master McCall and Sister Nell," consisting of an older girl, very flapper oriented and her little brother. The paper doll, proving successful with children used to amusing themselves creatively, was again issued later in the year with "Sister Nell Goes to a Party," and finally, in December 1925, the girl acquired the name "Betty." They again were highly successful, and served as an advertisement for patterns that were available from *McCall's* magazine. Serving two purposes, that of entertainment for children and advertising for adults, the pages of paper doll fun caught on.

By the beginning of the 1940s, World War II had given women another look at home sewing as war shortages forced some of the Industrial Revolution advances backward. In February 1943, a mother was added to the family, and teen model, *Peggy McCall* made her debut. *Peggy* was the first doll in the long series of McCall dolls, and with her movie star hair and figure, came packaged with fabrics and

*Barbie®* is the registered trademark of Mattel Toys, Inc.

trims and patterns. She was made by the Dritz-Traum Company, in a 13in (33cm) size, with only detachable arms. This author has even seen a deluxe model with a full-length mink coat that would be the envy of any would-be movie queen of the period.

Ironically, the debut of *Betsy McCall* on the cover of *McCall's* magazine in May 1951, showed the soon-to-be-familiar *Betsy* with a child model named Peggy McGregor, coincidentally uniting *Betsy* and "Peggy" as cover girls!

*Betsy* was introduced as a young girl going on six, and was kept at that age for around 22 years. When she progressed to junior high school age it was discovered that youngsters were STILL cutting out *Betsy McCall* paper dolls long after other toys were laid aside. High school girls, having grown up with *Betsy*, were putting her pictures on their mirrors, clinging to something "safe" from their childhood while trying to survive the perils of "teendom," a relatively new American life-style. While *Betsy* was created for fun, she served as an advertisement vehicle not only for McCall's patterns, one of the largest corporations in the business, but also to advertise many of the

**Illustration 2.** Another version of the 14in (36cm) *Betsy McCall* doll by Ideal. She is wearing red polished cotton and is a mint-in-box doll.

**BELOW: Illustration 3.** Close-up of the McCall's wrist tag with curlers on the Ideal doll, shown in *Illustration 2*. The drawing is just like *Betsy* appeared in *McCall's* magazine.

**Illustration 4.** 8in (20cm) *Betsy McCall* deluxe set, "Fashion Design Studio." Set includes all hard plastic doll and materials for additional outfits. This is a charming addition to a *Betsy* collection.

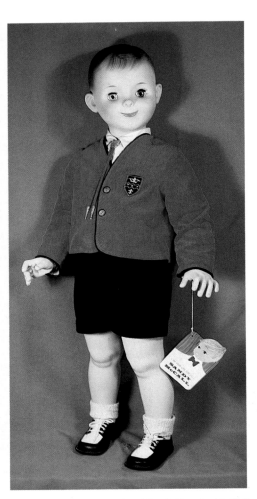

"miracle" fibers such as Dacron, nylon and rayon. These fibers were viewed cautiously at first by a public un-accustomed to synthetics, but sooned changed the way an entire nation dressed for nearly 30 years, until recently when designers have us back at the ironing board with the return of natural fibers!

Through advertising, manufacturers could use an established safe "star," as it were, to convince mom that her little darling would not be short-changed in a dress of easy care. Even the dolls of the period were beginning to come with labels stating: "My dress is of Dupont Nylon...and stays party pretty!" Through *Betsy McCall* advertisers had a reliable spokesperson. Backed also by *Parents' Magazine* and the Good Housekeeping Seal of Approval, synthetics and *Betsy McCall* were as American as Sunday School!

*Betsy* was also used to advertise her various franchises and licensed products,

and in September 1952, her first doll likeness, made by Ideal was introduced. Soon the concept was expanded so that some issues included *Betsy* showing arts and crafts, such as July 1956, where *Betsy* makes a hollyhock doll. Other lessons such as "How to Plant a Rose Garden," October 1956, and "Betsy Makes Her Own Puppets," January 1957, gave *Betsy McCall* a versatility unthought-of before. In 1958, almost every month had a theme, and catchy titles such as "Betsy Makes a Calender" (January) and "Betsy Looks for Easter Eggs" (April) exemplified the American dream of child-hood innocence that the public wanted so desperately to believe. Television shows such as "The Donna Reed Show" and "Father Knows Best" had idealized the American family as never before, and *Betsy McCall*, being a fictitious creation not subject to illnesses or temper tantrums, fit the mold to exact specification! Always proper, polite

**Illustration 5.** 38in (97cm) *Sandy McCall* by American Character, 1961. Wrist tag states he can wear real little boy's clothes. Made of top quality vinyl, he has molded hair and sleep eyes. *Gidget Donnelly Collection.*

**Illustration 6.** Extremely rare 36in (91cm) *Linda McCall* by American Character, circa 1961. This doll is often confused with *Betsy McCall*, but the hair style is slightly different. Her original price of $19.99 is on her box! *Gidget Donnelly Collection.*

**Illustration 7.** 14in (36cm) version of *Betsy McCall*, 1958, by American Character Doll Corp; all premium vinyl, jointed five-piece body; marked "McCall Corp" in a circle; she has rooted saran hair and sleep eyes. Her original dress and box add to her value.

**Illustration 8.** 29in (74cm) new *Betsy McCalls*, 1961. Billed as a three-dimensional paper doll, this version was used for the paper doll pages for a few months in 1962. The doll is rigid vinyl with rooted hair in a choice of colors and sleep eyes. *Colleen Giles Collection.*

and respectful, she was a role model of perfection that today we idealize as part of our past.

*Betsy's* artist in the early 1950s was Kay Morrissey, of *McCall's* staff, but in 1958 artist Ginnie Hofmann was assigned the task of drawing the little girl, her friends and family. From 1960 on, Selma Robinson of *McCall's* answered the thousands of letters *Betsy* received every year, always tactfully saying that, "*Betsy* has asked me to tell you..." instead of pretending to be *Betsy* herself. Soon other members of the *McCall's* staff joined in as imaginative trips by *Betsy* to Europe opened all sorts of possibilities for recipes and adventures. Interestingly, *Betsy* was a brunette, mainly because so were most little girls. *McCall's* research quickly learned that blonde hair may be the American ideal, but in reality only 10 percent of the population is fair-haired. With *Betsy* as a brunette, she could be more of a real friend to all. The company policy was that *Betsy* be "light and fluffy," on good terms with her parents, and, most important of all, be believable. If *Betsy McCall* liked

something, or wanted something, it was worth having.

The paper doll proved so successful that soon boxed sets were available through the mail for a surprisingly modest fee. Most of the memorable ones were made by Saalfield into the 1960s, and later by Whitman. Despite the three-dimensional dolls by Ideal and American Character and others, the paper dolls remained popular.

In June 1952, *Betsy's* stuffed duck was lost in the tide, and Nosy, her dog rescued it, but *Betsy* declared she wanted a real doll to play with, and one that "looks just like me!" By September, the Ideal doll was announced with paper version of *Betsy's* doll wearing three dresses in the magazine. The same issue had a three-page story on how the doll was made. Using the *Toni* doll body, a soft vinyl head with watermelon grin was utilized; a glued-on wig in *Betsy's* famous pageboy added to her charm. The doll was 14in (36cm) tall and sculpted by Bernard Lipfert. She came with a pinafore pattern, wrist tag with curlers and one of the three dresses shown on the paper doll. The

styles were either red polished cotton trimmed in white, gingham plaid with pinafore or white with flowers in print. The price was $7.95. The doll was immediately well received, and less imaginative children could now see their heroine in the "flesh," while the highly creative child could now relive *Betsy's* paper adventures with her own little friend. Soon the patterns were increased to tie in with the doll, and the name "Betsy McCall" became more of a household word than ever.

Because she appeared in an adult magazine, the link between mother and daughter gave advertisers a unique bond missing today, with so many toys advertised soley through children's shows and magazines. Of course, in the 1950s, it was more the parent who selected what the child would play with and not the child, so this tie-in was perfect!

With the entry of Vogue *Ginny* dolls into the marketplace, suddenly the popularity of larger dolls began to wane. The 8in (20cm) size dolls were the new "in" thing, and *Ginny* was capturing a lion's share of the doll

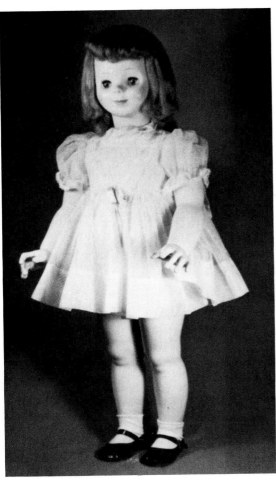

**LEFT: Illustration 9.** 36in (91cm) 1959 *Betsy McCall* by American Character, redressed. This doll was popular as a "companion doll" for a child to take with her! She is marked "McCall Corp" on her head. *Colleen Giles Collection.*

**RIGHT: Illustration 10.** 22in (56cm) *Betsy McCall*, unmarked, by American Character, all original. This doll features jointed ankles. *Colleen Giles Collection.*

market. (Note: For more information on *Ginny* and the Vogue doll story, see *Ginny...An American Toddler Doll*, A. Glenn Mandeville, Hobby House Press, Inc.) By 1957, most dolls sold were in the new smaller size. Another company, American Character of New York, was licensed to make a charming 8in (20cm) version of *Betsy McCall*. This doll was all hard plastic, with saran hair and a bisque-like finish which, like that of *Ginny*, was indestructible. She was first introduced with 18 costume changes, at a basic cost of $2.25, with additional costumes priced from $1.50 to $3.00 each. This was soon followed by three deluxe sets, a designer's studio, a dude ranch and a day with *Betsy*. Also packaged with the doll was a wonderful comic book, drawn 1950s style, that showed little girls playing with *Betsy McCall*. Soon other deluxe sets were introduced such as "Day at the Beach" and "Betsy McCall's Garden." Each included a doll and extra clothing.

By 1958, slightly bigger dolls were being shown at Toy Fair. American Character introduced a 14in (36cm) size *Betsy* with a trunk and extra clothes. By 1959, a 20in (51cm) version

was made. These dolls were lovely, in a rich creamy vinyl for which American Character was known. Some had fancy dresses, even wedding gowns for imaginative play; the better dolls had flirty eyes. *Betsy McCall* was THE doll in the Sears, Roebuck and Co. catalog of 1960!

By 1961, *McCall's* wondered if the whole *Betsy McCall* image might seriously be in need of an update. The world was interested in CHANGE in the early 1960s, both socially, and economically. *McCall's* announced in the editorial pages, December 1961, that a 29in (74cm) American Character *Betsy McCall* doll would be photographed and used for *Betsy's* adventures rather than a drawn paper doll. This, the editorial stated, would give *Betsy* three-dimensional adventures that more types of youngsters could enjoy. The doll was issued in stores in blonde, golden blonde, brunette or red hair, and with brown or blue eyes. She was definitely a departure from the traditional *Betsy McCall*, and was aimed at selecting a *Betsy* doll who looked like the child. This, in my opinion, weakened the image of *Betsy* as a brunette with brown eyes, and made

her just another doll.

*McCall's* advertised the doll in all hair colors, but a blonde was selected for *Betsy's* adventures, adding again to the displacement of her identity. Popular opinion thankfully came to the rescue, and by April 1962, the traditional *Betsy* was back in paper doll form.

By this time, "companion dolls," or life-size walking dolls had become all the rage with children. Everywhere, tots could be seen lugging behind them a doll often bigger than themselves! It was a big change for the doll manufacturers, after years of smaller dolls. American Character responded to this need by issuing a 36in (91cm) doll of *Betsy McCall* and *Linda McCall*, her cousin and tripmate on many adventures. Soon after came 38in (97cm) *Sandy McCall*, a large companion boy doll perhaps aimed at little boys who, after all these years, must have been jealous of the relationship between their sisters and *Betsy*. With *Sandy*, a boy had his own "buddy" to talk to and, in many ways, dolls like this were the forerunners of boys' "action figures" and "buddy" type dolls, new on the market recently.

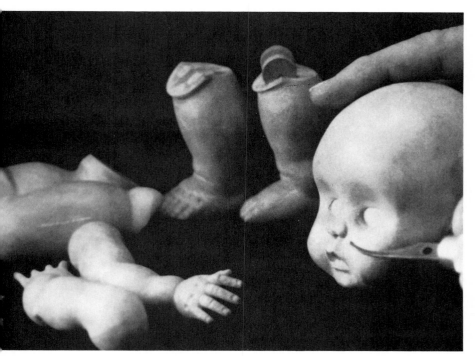

**Illustration 11.** Sculpting of the new Rothschild *Betsy McCall* doll. It took 43 different people to make this doll. She is made much like the doll of the late 1950s. *Photograph courtesy of Rothschild Doll Company.*

BETSY McCALL

— A friend of mothers and their daughters for 35 years —

troducing
e
th Anniversary
tsy McCall
oll
llection

The New Standard —
ROTHSCHILD
DOLL COMPANY
Southboro, MA 01772
(617) 481-3400

NEW FOR 1986! 8-inch size in hard-plastic with bending-knee joint. Traditional strung construction. Also available in 12-inch size.

**Illustration 12.** Advertisement for the new 1986 version of *Betsy McCall* unveiled at Toy Fair by the Rothschild Doll Company. As one can see from the photograph, much attention to detail is being used. This doll captures the innocence of the early *Betsy* dolls.

Nothing ever remains the same, and in 1964 *McCall's* again felt the need to create a new *Betsy* image. This time the Uneeda doll company made an 11½in (29cm) doll, more in line with the fashion dolls of the period such as *Barbie®* and *Tammy*. Shown for $2.99 in the 1964 Sears, Roebuck and Co. catalog, she had reddish hair. The doll was introduced in *McCall's* magazine in August 1964 by Carol Channing. I feel this doll is lovely, and is yet undiscovered by most collectors. She really captures the new junior high school age of *Betsy*. The Carol Channing tie-in was tastefully done, with a poster of Carol saying, "Hello, Dolly" to the new *Betsy McCall!*

*Betsy* again was in full swing, with big names like Shari Lewis, the popular ventriloquist, having the dolls as a regular advertiser. Together with this, of course, came the onslaught of licensed products that ranged from overnight cases to cologne, and the ever present patterns for little girls and their dolls. Some interesting licenses were children's dishes showing *Betsy* and Nosy, a cookie cutter in the image of *Betsy* and a Model's Hat Box, filled with cosmetics to keep a little girl glamorous. Last but not least were *Betsy* storybooks, and even a record and singing album, leaving collectors with a bounty of *Betsy McCall* collectibles.

Finally, in the 1970s, Horsman purchased a license to do a McCall doll, but, as was the custom of the 1970s, standard dolls from the line

were used and just named *Betsy McCall*. The character as we know it was gone. In the late 1970s, a bizarre taller teen-type doll was issued. Times were changing. The magazine had chosen to all but discontinue the paper doll as this current generation could hardly get excited over a paper doll of a young girl finding sea gull feathers on the beach! It was truly the end of an era.

Today, however, the children known as "baby boomers" who grew up with *Betsy McCall*, are worried that the pendulum has swung too far. They think perhaps some of the values taught to them were not so wrong after all. Maybe in the 1980s a little more politeness, consideration and feeling is what is needed after the decade of "me" in the 1970s. This generation of mothers is ready for their daughters to have some choices. Maybe not everyone is suited to bake cookies and change diapers as we were taught in the 1950s, but neither is every woman ready to be an astronaut. Today, CHOICE is the word. *Betsy McCall* and the values she taught are again becoming popular. Add to that the fact that adults remember her nostalgically, and that adds up to a new *Betsy McCall*.

The Rothschild Doll Company, in a licensing agreement with *McCall's*, has again captured the innocence and sweetness of *Betsy*. Their charming new 8in (20cm) doll, to be followed by other sizes, captures the old look of *Betsy*. Made just like the old hard plastic dolls, this new version is dressed in the same type of fabrics, and has a glued-on wig. It is a tribute to modern doll making to create a new doll that looks so much like the past.

Yes, *Betsy McCall* has come full circle. The values she taught are ones of lasting character. Looking to the past as well as the future, we can take the lessons *Betsy* taught us and apply them to today. *Betsy McCall* is a classic, and one that we hope will always be with us. A memory of the past, a presence of the future, she will always represent the ideals we as humans strive to achieve.

Acknowledgments: The author would like to thank Loraine Burdick for background information, *McCall's* magazine for the use of their archives, Colleen Giles and Gidget Donnelly for allowing me to photograph rare dolls, Bob Gantz for helping with photographs and Kathi Van Laar for coordinating this project. □

# The *Chatty Cathy* Story

When one thinks of "Mattel," naturally one's mind immediately focuses on the world-famous *Barbie®* doll! Yet this innovative company, founded in a garage in 1945, had another series of dolls that today are highly collectible and worthy of study, namely the "Chatty Series."

I have always felt that an interesting collection that a doll collector might want to assemble would be that of a selection of dolls that represent children from the turn of the century on. One could include the beautiful Kämmer & Reinhardt character children such as *Gretchen* and *Marie*, so expressive with their pouty looks, and the pensive Käthe Kruse dolls which so resembled German children. Naturally one would want the *American Children* created by Dewees Cochran during the 1930s as well.

As for representing typical children in the 1940s, Madame Alexander's *Wendy-Ann* would, of course, be in the collection, and in the 1950s, Effanbee's *Honey* and Ideal's *Toni* would certainly represent the child of their decade.

When one gets to the 1960s, choices of dolls that really look like the children of their decade dwindle as mass manufacturing took its toll on creativity. Blank face dolls with different wigs and clothing beckoned from store shelves with almost lifeless stares, but one doll stands out from all

*LEFT: Illustration 1. By 1961, another hair style, nicknamed "dog ears" after the floppy cocker spaniel ears (the dog of the boom children) was added. The rich heavy vinyl makes* Chatty Cathy® *a high quality doll. The clothing is finely tailored like real garments.*

*RIGHT: Illustration 2. Here is one case where the original box adds much to the history of the doll. The box is rich in nostalgic views of childhood in the early 1960s.*

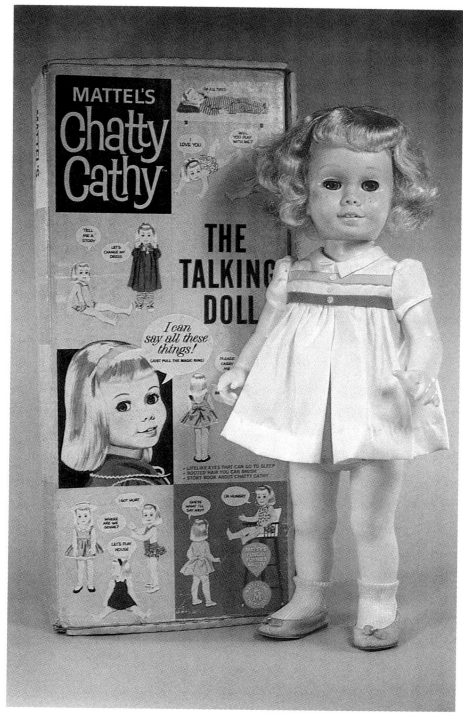

**Illustration 3.** *A VERY rare black* Chatty Cathy®. *These dolls were not widely distributed and are very difficult to find today. They are worth about $300 in mint condition.*

**Illustration 4.** *Full-length view of the black* Chatty Cathy®, *seen in* Illustration 3, *showing the body proportions and hand movements. These dolls captured children at their loving best.*

the others, and that is *Chatty Cathy*®!

Recently, with all the publicity concerning Ruth and Elliot Handler (they were the recipients of the prestigious DOTY Lifetime Achievement Award in 1987), founders of Mattel, and the fact that there are currently several books about *Barbie*® on the market, including one by this author, several individuals have come forward claiming to have "designed" both *Barbie* and *Chatty Cathy*.

To put this in perspective, one must remember that in any company, not just Mattel, there is usually a design "team" that works on a concept suggested by the owner. Just as in the garment industry, the toy industry operates on this sytem as well. Even the Alexander Doll Company has had other designers working along with Madame Alexander (this author has interviewed several of them over the years) to create the lovely dolls for which this company is famous.

One thing I am sure of...Ruth Handler is an unbelievably talented individual who possessed an uncanny knowledge of what would please the public, and *Chatty Cathy*, her second most famous doll, did just that!

In my opinion, the lukewarm reception which *Barbie* received in 1959, made the Handlers reevaluate whether Americans really wanted such a sophisticated doll as *Barbie* or whether "traditional" dolls were still the answer.

*Chatty Cathy* was truly unique in several ways. First, her face resembled that of a typical American child, not one that could model children's fashions in *McCalls* or *Ladies' Home Journal*, but the type of little girl one ran into daily at the supermarket, Sunday School or in a playground. Her slightly buck teeth told of future orthodontics work needed (that is, "braces," the status symbol of the boom children), and her hair was longish and straight. Her body typified the ice cream indulged child with the slightly protruding tummy, while her hands were posed creatively. All in all, *Chatty Cathy* represented, as did those previously-mentioned dolls before her, the ordinary adorable child of her day, the early 1960s.

Adding to the play value of this doll was an outstanding new development, a pull string that gave *Chatty Cathy* the ability to "chat," or speak several phrases. Innocent charming banter came out of a cloth-covered speaker in the early dolls that asked, "Please play with me," or "Please brush my hair."

All of these phrases were designed to convey the "helpless" state that *Chatty Cathy* was in when found at the store (sort of like a puppy just waiting for a new owner).

This fulfilled perfectly the stereotype image of the word "doll" during the past several decades. A helpless little waif that needed a "mommy" to take care of her, and at the same time, nurture that "mother" instinct that some say is inborn to all females (though many today question such a general statement). Through playing with dolls, a little girl would learn how to prepare for the future, perhaps the ONLY future she would ever be offered. In my opinion, dolls today (even doll artist dolls) that are historical or educational or even glamorous, still suffer from the stereotyped image

*Illustration 5. Original advertisement for* Chatty Cathy® *shown in* Toys and Novelties *for March 1960. The ad states the phrases that* Chatty Cathy® *can "chat." The bottom of the ad shows the price as $18.00 retail! Also available was a dolls' house store display.*

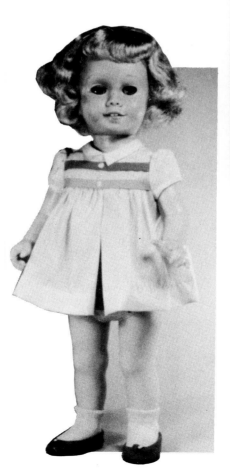

*Illustration 6. Interesting "extras" were available for the* Chatty Cathy® *dolls, such as this rare bed, made by Susy Goose Company which made all the* Barbie® *furniture.*

*Illustration 7. A full length view of the* Chatty Cathy® *shown in color in* Illustration 2.

*Illustration 8.* Collectors are always on the lookout for rare versions of Chatty Cathy® such as this doll which features side-glancing eyes and dark freckles. A collection can consist of hundreds of different examples just like Barbie®. It is amazing that so many variations exist in mass manufactured dolls.

*Illustration 9.* Full view of side-glancing Chatty Cathy® showing high quality sandals and protruding tummy, the sign of a "well-fed well-cared-for child."

*Illustration 10.* Made from the Chatty Cathy® molds, Chatty Baby® was designed to be a younger member of the family.

of a little girl playing mommy to her doll, thus making collecting dolls difficult to explain to many to whom the word "doll" implies only one type of image.

As 1960 progressed and *Barbie* caught on greatly with the public, *Chatty Cathy* succeeded in her own right as the alter ego of the child. *Barbie* represented the future, while *Chatty Cathy* represented the present.

Additional wardrobe sets were available for the doll. Beautifully made, many used the same fabrics as the *Barbie* outfits from that period! All of the ensembles focused on childhood, with Sunday School outfits, after school playwear and school dresses high on the list. Rounding out the wardrobe were pajama sets and even a bed! Collectors today that adore *Chatty Cathy* seem to be those that were her age (about five to eight years old in 1960) and see themselves in her. The second group of collectors are the parents of these children, often today in their 60s, whose daughters now are sophisticated icons of *Vogue* magazine! *Chatty Cathy* reminds these women of the little girl they once knew, who depended on mommy to brush her hair and take care of her.

The "Chatty Series" was so successful that other dolls were added to the line. *Chatty Baby*, made from the same body mold as *Chatty Cathy* was a big seller, and a *Chatty Brother* and *Sister* joined the family in 1961 to 1962 as did *Tiny Chatty Baby* and rare black versions of some of these dolls.

Interestingly, blacks did not see *Chatty Cathy* as black. She was part of the "American Dream" at the time, and for most, unfortunately, unless you were white, with a name you could pronounce, social acceptance was just not there. Fantasy play was popular among those who could never be accepted, and dolls offered an escape.

I do not profess to be an expert on the "Chatty Series" of dolls. I only like what they represent: a little girl needing nurturing and care, that looks like what many think a child should look like. Many collectors specialize in this type of doll and can tell you all the mold numbers and subtle differences and year-to-year changes. I cannot. All I can do is acquaint you, through beautiful photographs, with a

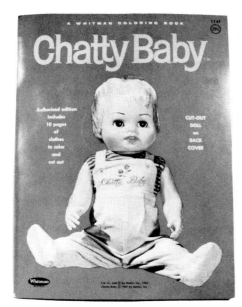

**Illustration 11.** *Many paper products were available for the "Chatty Series" such as this coloring book by Whitman. Other items included sticker fun books and paper dolls.*

**Illustration 12.** *A Golden Book featuring Charmin' Chatty® (about whom an entire article could be written). Charmin' Chatty® was the 1963 addition to the family and represented a pre-teenager. Collectors fondly remember these dolls as a happy part of their lives.*

**Illustration 13.** *Highly sought-after are the* Tiny Chatty Brother® *and* Sister®. *Smaller and more petite, they conveyed the "little child" concept to the hilt.*

dear doll friend of mine that you may want to make yours as well!

*Chatty Cathy* represents to me "Trisha," the little girl taken in as an orphan by the Stones on "The Donna Reed Show" in 1963, and played by Patty Petersen (real-life sister of Paul Petersen, Jeff Stone on the show and one of the original Mouseketeers); a child that we all can love and adore caught forever in doll form. Why not adopt *Chatty Cathy* the next time you

see one that needs a new home? □
Authors note: *Chatty Cathy* dolls, because they were so mass manufactured, today are seldom priced over $50 unless they are in mint condition. Dolls in boxes can fetch $200 if perfect with wrist tags. Most dolls no longer talk but can be repaired. The most valuable dolls are the black versions of the different family members. *Chatty Cathy* is still one of the real doll bargains around today!

The author would like to thank the following collectors for providing dolls and other material to the author: Franklin Lim Liao for the original *Chatty Cathy* ads; Mrs. John Thomas, Thelma Elias, Barb Drake, Dick Tahsin and Janet Jillson, your help is greatly appreciated!

*Barbie®, Chatty Cathy®, Chatty Baby®, Chatty Brother® and Sister®, Tiny Chatty Baby®, Tiny Chatty Brother® and Sister® and Charmin' Chatty®* are registered trademarks of Mattel, Inc.

# The Mary Hartline Story.....

Part of the fun of writing doll books and articles is in uncovering new information. Sometimes, this new knowledge leads a collector into fields that are off the subject of dolls, but extremely informative and interesting.

One of the aspects of doll collecting I find fascinating is learning where a doll fits into history. In other words, what was going on in our culture that inspired this creation; what story does it tell for us and future generations about our past and the way we lived.

When reviewing prices for *The Celebrity Doll Price Guide and Annual* by John Axe and A. Glenn Mandeville, Hobby House Press, Inc., I found myself asking, who is Mary Hartline, and what made her famous? Even though I was a child in the 1950s, I did not remember much about her. Her story is one similar to many celebrities of the period, one that would not change until the 1980s when beautiful women like Joan Collins would not "retire" at age 30 and never be heard from again.

In 1949, television was a relatively new medium. Black and white images of live shows and the views they represented were beamed into American homes for the first time. Americans, used to only hearing dramatic programs, and using their imaginations to conjure up the action, were now bombarded by shows that featured "entertainment," presentations that did not have dramatic content but were visual in their format. The "variety" show came into being. It was a novel experience where a viewer could simply be "entertained" while performers juggled, sang, danced or performed some other stunt that made the audience watch the magic box and the images it contained.

**Illustration 1.** Truly a masterpiece of the "Golden Age" of dolls, this 24in (61cm) Ideal *Mary Hartline* is unique in that her neck is part of the head, making it swivel. She is marked "P-94" on her back. Constructed of all hard plastic, she has a glued-on wig, sleep eyes and wears a satin-taffeta dress with silk screened design. Her wrist tag announces that she is "The Pretty Princess of TV."

Many early telecasts, such as "Show of Shows," featured a variety of acts designed to be visual in nature. In 1949, a Chicago, Illinois, television station premiered "Super Circus" on Sunday evenings. The hostess of the show was a lovely voluptuous blonde named Mary Hartline. Her looks were wholesome, yet just this side of sexy. Dressed in a red and white majorette type outfit, Mary Hartline introduced each of the acts on this live variety show. Her platinum looks capitalized on the public's fascination with Marilyn Monroe, yet she had family appeal. It was a perfect match and one that is still hard to find today.

Soon "Super Circus" became too big to be housed in Chicago. In 1952, the show relocated to New York, New York, and acquired Jerry Cologna, a semi-celebrity of the 1950s as host. His "Ed Sullivan" type personality, coupled with the flamboyant Mary Hartline was an unbeatable combination. Mary became irresistible to the American public. Her image spawned a raft of "imitations" such as Sally Starr, a local Philadelphia, Pennsylvania, television personality. (For a close-up of a *Sally Starr* doll, see Winter 1984, *Doll Values Quarterly,* Hobby House Press, Inc.). Sally Starr, not quite as young, or as sexy or innocent as her predecessor, announced everyday to a generation of tots that they "sure looked good to your gal Sal." Sally, also a victim of the "washed up at 40" philosophy that drove Norma Shearer and Deanna Durbin to seclusion in Paris, France, recently has made a comeback in the Philadelphia area, and is in demand again.

Mary Hartline can be called a fancy "showgirl." Her majorette outfit and twirling baton earned her a contract in the mid 1950s with Canada Dry

**TOP: Illustration 2.** This 16in (40.6cm) *Mary Hartline* is made from the P-91 *Toni* doll molds. She is a strung doll, although later dolls were walkers. The durability of these early 1950s all hard plastic dolls make them the future antiques of their generation.

**BOTTOM: Illustration 3.** End of doll box for doll seen in *Illustration 2.* Ideal dared to use Mary Hartline's picture with her holding one of the dolls. The likeness is uncanny considering no special molds were used. Ideal's boxes were interesting and add much to the value of their dolls.

Ginger Ale as its official spokeswoman. Like Joan Crawford had done for Lux soap, Mary Hartline gave an air of celebrity status to a quite ordinary product, a soft drink. Her ads captured a vivacious innocence that today is refreshing.

Like most celebrities of her day, Mary Hartline realized that the party would soon be over. Our culture at the time worshipped youth, and few female "stars" could and would stand the test of time. Most chose to retire gracefully, and live off their past incomes, rather than be ousted out by a younger prettier face.

**LEFT: Illustration 4.** Ideal also made this colorful box to house its smallest 8in (20.3cm) doll. This is truly a case where the box is as interesting as the doll.

**BELOW: Illustration 5.** *Mary Hartline* dolls came in various colored dresses such as the green dress shown here. Other colors were navy blue, and the reverse colors such as red lettering on white background. Cottons and satins were used. The small dress differs from the dress on the doll in *Illustration 4.* It is for the doll made by another company (possibly Virga, although not substantiated), and is subtly different.

**Illustration 6.** Canada Dry Ginger Ale advertisement, circa 1953. Mary Hartline's wholesome good looks, coupled with her obvious charms, made her a natural for an all-American product such as Canada Dry!

Toy companies, namely Ideal, secured the contract to manufacture *Mary Hartline* dolls in several sizes. Made during the "golden age" of dolls, these hard plastic wonders are among the fastest rising dolls in popularity with collectors. Ideal made these dolls, using the *Toni* doll molds, with such realism, that the wrist tags actually showed Mary holding one of the dolls next to her. Despite the fact that no special mold was used, the resemblance is uncanny, and truly captures what the star stood for.

Finally, in 1956, the show went off

the air. Mary Hartline, born in 1926, was now 30 years old. Determined to use her blonde good looks in another way, she married millionaire Woolworth Donahue, and "retired" to Palm Beach, Florida. Similar to many of the movie queens of her era, Mary Hartline wanted nothing to do with her past life. Like Loretta Young, she attempted to stay out of the public eye rather than be compared at age 50 to her youthful formal images. Another victim of the "youth cult," Mary refused to grant interviews. It is unknown today what she is doing with her life, but the

pattern of her seclusion is similar to the great and not-so-great "stars" of her period.

Many celebrities of the past are being kept alive by doll collectors who worship the images created in their likenesses. For many of us, "The Pretty Princess of TV" will live on in our hearts forever. (For more information on Mary Hartline, see *The Encyclopedia of Celebrity Dolls* by John Axe. For values on *Mary Hartline* dolls, consult *The Celebrity Doll Price Guide and Annual,* John Axe and A. Glenn Mandeville, Hobby House Press, Inc.) □

# INDEX

**A**

*Agatha* 170
*Aja* 63, 64, 67
Alexander Doll Company 82, 84, 106, 182
*Alexander-Kins* 84, 142, 168
*Allan* 45
American Character 52, 60, 136, 178
*American Children* 181
*American Girl Barbie* 23
*American Girl Bendable Leg Barbie* 18
Annalee Doll Company 132
Annette Funicello 25
*Apple Annie* 170
Arranbee 52

**B**

Barbara Britton 149
*Barbie* 6, 13, 14, 15, 17, 34, 45, 115, 116, 132, 133, 136, 140, 153, 157, 172, 174, 179, 181, 182
*Barbie and the Rockers* 34
*Barbie and the Rockers Barbie* 46
*Barbie and the Rockers Ken* 46
*Barbie Goes to College* 19
*Barbie Hair Fair* 39
*Barbie's Best Friend, Midge* 35
*Barbie's Cousin, Francie* 27
*Barbie's Friendship* 41
*Barbie's MODern Cousin Francie* 32, 159
*Bendable Leg Barbie* 20, 21, 36
*Bendable Leg Skipper* 21
*Betsy McCall* 136, 174, 175, 176, 178, 179
*Betty* 172
*Billy Boy Barbie* 35
Birnbaum, William *83*
*Black Barbie* 117, 119
Bob Mackie 123, 125
*Brad* 34
Britton, Barbara 149
Brooke Shields 79
*Brooke Shields* 78, 81
*Bye Bye Baby* 167

**C**

*Cabbage Patch Kids* 84, 112, 113, 162
*California Barbie* 35
*California Christie* 118

*Candy Pop Barbie* 8
Carlson, Virginia Graves 140
*Casey* 151, 159
*Charlie's Angels* 95
*Charmin' Chatty* 135
*Chatty Baby* 184
*Chatty Brother and Sister* 184
*Chatty Cathy* 182, 183, 184, 185
*Chatty Series* 184
Cher 121, 122, 123
*Cher* 120, 127
*Cheri* 170
Chodorow, Jeff *83, 84*
*Christie* 28, 34, 35, 45, 49, 116
*Cinderella* 171
*Cissette* 170
*Cissy* 149, 153, 170
*Clash* 66
Coleco 112
*Color Magic Barbie* 23
*Court Jester* 145
Couture Period 16, 20, 23
*Curlylocks* 170
*Cynthia* 115

**D**

*Daddy's Girl* 164
Dakin Company 102, 106, 143
*Dallas* 34
*Danse* 71
*Darci* 69
*Deanna Durbin* 147, 162
*Derek* 35
*Deux-L* 88, 91
*Dewees Cochran* 51, 130, 181
Diana Ross 115, 118
Dionne Quintuplets 84, 87

**E**

*Easter Doll* 173
Effanbee 51, 102, 110, 164
*Elesse* 119
Emilio Pucci 41
*Emmet Benton* 63
*Erica* 137
Excelina Collection 6, 7

**F**

Fabares, Shelley 25
Faith Wick 106
Farrah Fawcett-Majors 33
*Fashion Queen Barbie* 21, 22, 44

Fawcett-Majors, Farrah 33
*First Ladies* 85
Fisher-girl 132
*Flo Jo* 116, 119
*Francie* 34, 45, 116, 156, 159
*Fruits Kiss Barbie* 8
Funicello, Annette 25
*Fun to Dress Barbie* 116

**G**

*Gay Parisienne* 11
*Gettin' Fancy Kimberly* 111, 112, 113
*G.I. Joe* 22
*Ginny* 102, 115, 139, 140, 142, 143, 144, 145, 164, 169, 178
*Gillette Company* 147
*Glitter 'N' Gold Jem* 74
*Gloria Ann* 130
*Godey Lady* 171
Graves, Jennie 139, 140, 145
*Gretchen* 181
*Groom* 169
*Growing Hair Cher* 127, 128

**H**

*Hair Fair Barbie* 26, 28, 38, 39
Handler 12, 14, 15, 16, 19, 22, 32, 73, 157
*Hansel & Gretel* 170
*Happy Holidays Barbie* 118
*Harriet Hubbard Ayer* doll 147
Hasbro Inc. 64, 68, 71, 77
*Hollywood Jem* 71, 76
Holograms, The 64, 69, 71
*Honey* 181
Hornby, Lesley 158
Hoyer, Mary 52
*Horseman* 179

**I**

Ideal 60, 107, 136, 140, 149, 153, 161, 162, 189
*International Barbies* 35
Ira Smith 83, 84

**J**

Jacqueline Kennedy 19, 23
*Japanese Kimono Barbie* 8
Jeff Chodorow 83, 84
*Jem* 63, 64, 66, 67, 68, 69, 71, 72
Jennie Graves 139, 140, 145

Jenny 59
Jerrica 63
JESCO 52, 53, 55
Jetta 66
Jim Skahill 52, 53
Joanie 164, 172
John F. Kennedy 19
Judy Garland doll 132, 147
Julia 116, 119
Just Me dolls 139

**K**
Kämmer & Reinhardt 181
Kansai Barbie 8
Katie 52, 53, 54, 55
Katie Keene 22
Katie Kollectables 54
Kennedy, Jacqueline 19, 23
Kennedy, John F. 19
Kelley 97
Ken 6, 16, 17, 27, 34, 45
Kenner 69, 95
Ken's Buddy Allen 22
Kimber 63, 64
Kimberly 110, 113

**L**
Lady Luminous 88, 91, 92, 94
Ladybird Johnson 19
Lavender Surprise Barbie 118
'Legends" 52
Lesley Hornby 158
Lesney Company 144
Licca 58, 94
Linda 139
Linda McCall 176, 178
Little Madaline 169
Little Miss Renee 152, 153
Little Miss Revlon 149, 151, 152
Lisa 58, 94
Little Southern Girl 169
Live Action Barbie 31
Living Barbie 6, 32
Living Eli 6
LJN Toys, Ltd 81
Lori Martin 166

**M**
Mackie, Bob 123, 125
Madame Alexander 20, 51, 52, 60, 69, 82, 83, 84, 105, 107, 110, 130, 149, 162, 164, 168
Magic Curl Barbie 118
Maggie 84
Malibu Barbie 28, 32
Marie 181

Marilyn Monroe 137
Mary Hartline 107, 147, 186, 187, 188, 189
Mary Hoyer 52
Mary Jane 164
Mary Louise 169, 170
Mary Quant 27
Marx Company 41
Mattel 19, 23, 25, 26, 28, 31, 45, 68, 80, 99, 115, 116, 117, 134, 140, 157, 181
Maxi 72, 77
McCall's magazine 174, 175, 177, 179
Melanie 170
Midge 15, 16, 17, 22, 45
Minx 71, 76
Misfits,The 66, 67, 68, 69, 71
Miss Ginny of 1987 145
Miss Ideal 167
Miss Seventeen...A Beauty Queen 134

**N**
Nancy Villasenor 52
Naomi 117, 119
New Kids On The Block 106
Now Look Ken 31

**O**
Osmonds, Donny, Jimmy & Marie 33

**P**
Patty Pease 110
Patty Playpal 134, 153, 161, 166
Pease, Patty 110
Peggy McCall 174, 175
Penny Playpal 163, 164
Peter Pan 169
Peter Playpal 162, 163
Petite Mannequin 88
Petite Patti 166
Pink Jubilee 35
Pizazz 66, 67
Playpal Series 140
Portrettes 84
Portrait Dolls 51
Prince 31
Princess Mary 147, 149
Prom Party Brooke Shields 79, 80
Pucci, Emilio 41

**Q**
Quiz-Kin Bride 169

**R**
R. John Wright 102
Raggedy Ann 107
Rapture 71
Raynal dolls 131
Regine Lesaré 77
Revlon 107, 132, 140, 146, 147, 148, 150, 151, 153
Rhett 106
Ricky 23
Rio Pachecco 63, 65
Riot 71
Rob 77
Rock 'N' Curl Jem 64
Rocker Ken 35
Rockers,The 68
Romantic Barbie 6, 7, 8, 9
Romeo & Juliet 170
Ross, Diana 115, 118
Roxy 66
Ruth & Elliot Handler 12, 14, 15, 16, 19, 22, 32, 43, 45, 157, 182, 183

**S**
Sally Starr 187
Sandy McCall 176, 178
Sara Ann 133
Sara Lee 115
Sari Sasha doll 102
Sasha doll 102, 110
Saucy Walker 164
Scarlett 106, 170, 172
Shana Elmsferg 63, 64, 67
Shaun 95, 97, 98, 99, 100
Shelley Fabares 25
Shields, Brooke 79
Shirley Temple doll 130, 147, 161, 162
Shirley Temple Playpal 164
Skahill, Jim 52, 53
Skipper, Barbie's Little Sister 22, 32, 45, 116, 118
Skooter 23
Smith, Ira 83, 84
So-Lite babies 133
Sonny and Cher 124
Sonny and Cher dolls 126
Southern Belle 170, 173
Starlight House Foster Girls 65
Starr 95, 97, 98, 99, 100, 101
Starr...and Her High School Friends 97
Starr, Sally 187
Steffie 45
Stingers 71, 72, 76
Stormer 66

*Suntan Brooke Shields* 79, 81
*Superstar Barbie* 6, 7, 33, 95
*Superstar Ken* 33
*Suzy Playpal* 164
*Sweet Country Barbie* 6, 7
*Sweet 16 Barbie* 32
*Sweet Sue* 107, 132, 149
*Sweet Sue Sophisticate* 149
*Swirl Ponytail Barbie* 19

**T**
*Takara Barbie* 6
*Takara Barbie & Ken* 10
*Takara Doll Company* 6, 58, 60, 88, 91
*Talking Barbie* 26, 27
*Tammy* 116, 179
*Tinker Bell* 173
*Tiny Chatty Baby* 184
*Tiny Patti* 166
*Tiny Tears* 107
*Tippi* 105
*Todd* 45
*Tomy Corporation* 111
*Toni* 107, 132, 136, 147, 149, 181, 187
*Tracy* 45, 97, 100
*Tressy* 116
*Tutti* 45
*Twiggy* 27, 41, 155, 156, 158, 159, 160
*Twist 'N' Turn Barbie* 25, 49
*Twist 'N' Turn Francie* 29

**U**
*UNICEF Barbie* 119

**V**
*Victoria* 169
*Video* 72
Villasenor, Nancy 52
Virginia Graves Carlson 140
Vogue Doll Company 139, 140, 164, 169, 177

**W**
*Walk Lively Steffie* 49
*Wanda* 142
*Wendy* 171, 172
*Wendy Calls On A School Friend* 172
*Wendy-Ann* 168, 170, 172, 181
*Wendy-Kins* 172, 173
*Western Barbie* 34
William Birnbaum 83

World Doll 106, 137
Wright, R. John 102

**Y**
Yamomoto Kansai 8
*You* dolls 56, 57, 58, 59, 60, 61